ATOMS, ENERGY AND MACHINES

CREATIVE SCIENCE SERIES

Etta Schneider Ress, Ed.D., *editor-in-chief*
Gerhard Ramberg, *art editor*

PLANETS, STARS AND SPACE

Joseph Miles Chamberlain, Chief Astronomer
American Museum-Hayden Planetarium
Thomas D. Nicholson, Associate Astronomer

THE EARTH'S STORY

Gerald Ames and Rose Wyler
Authors, *The Golden Book of Astronomy, Restless Earth,
The Story of the Ice Age*

THE WAY OF THE WEATHER

Jerome Spar, Ph.D., Associate Professor
Department of Meteorology and Oceanography
New York University, N. Y.

ATOMS, ENERGY AND MACHINES

Jack McCormick, Ph.D.
The American Museum of Natural History, New York, N. Y.

ATOMS, ENERGY AND MACHINES

by

Jack McCormick

The American Museum of Natural History
New York

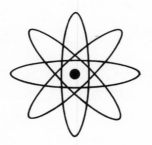

In Co-operation with

THE AMERICAN MUSEUM OF NATURAL HISTORY

N E W   Y O R K

Published by Creative Educational Society

1961
Printing

Illustrated by

Helmut Wimmer, American Museum-Hayden Planetarium, New York, N. Y.

ATOMS, ENERGY AND MACHINES

Copyright 1957 by
Creative Educational Society, Inc.
Mankato, Minnesota

*International copyrights
reserved in all countries*

PRINTED IN THE U.S.A.

Library of Congress Catalog Card Number 57-10398

Foreword

Science has come to be recognized as one of the dominant forces of our time. Because of its leading role in shaping our civilization, science must be brought to people everywhere.

There are many ways of practicing the dissemination of science, and several media through which this process can operate. As long as it remains accurate, sincere, and interesting, each approach to public education in this field has its legitimate place.

The printed word, aided and augmented by appropriate pictorial illustration, remains one of the best ways of carrying science to the public. In this book Dr. McCormick, through the medium of a hundred brief texts and numerous photographs and diagrams, presents a concise yet far-ranging survey of many aspects of our physical environment.

People want direct, simple answers to the many questions that arise in their minds as a result of the unprecedented scientific development and technical wizardry of the age in which they are living. *Atoms, Energy and Machines* will meet this need admirably as far as the physical world is concerned. It might be thought of as a first, informal introduction to physics and chemistry. As such, it treats many developments that are on the frontiers of these mushrooming sciences, yet it pays due attention to the more basic, if somewhat less spectacular topics which are fundamental to the later developments.

Clear, simple and forthright in method of presentation, this book should do much toward bringing science down to earth and thereby open new vistas of pleasurable enlightenment for the average person.

Ira M. Freeman
Rutgers, The State University
New Brunswick, N. J.

Contents

Contents (continued)

Introduction

Tomorrow's world, as new and different as it may be, will be built upon a foundation of knowledge laid by today's and by yesterday's worlds. This book is an introduction to our accumulated knowledge of chemistry and physics. It is written with the sincere hope that the young men and women who read it —citizens of tomorrow's world—will find in it the inspiration that will lead them to seek further into these basic sciences. Such a search will bring the lasting reward of understanding; understanding that will enrich their lives regardless of later choice of profession. Or, the search may lead to a career in science. Such a career will be exciting, satisfying, secure and, perhaps, supremely beneficial to all mankind.

This book is humbly dedicated to my son, Jamey, and to the other young citizens of our world. They will soon inherit the power to destroy and the responsibility to protect man and nature.

Jack McCormick

CHAPTER I

MATTER AND ITS BUILDING BLOCKS

ALL MATTER is composed of atoms. Groups of atoms are electrically bonded together to form molecules. And the molecules, in turn, may be held together by forces of mutual attraction, thereby joining to produce visible matter.

Once we have learned how matter is constructed, we will be better able to understand how it behaves, what happens when matter is burned, why some things float, how things move, and so on.

In this chapter you will see many objects that are familiar to you, but they will appear in a new light, as matter behaving according to the principles of physics.

THE WORLD OF THE ATOM

MORE THAN 24 centuries ago Greek philosophers discussed the possibility of dividing substances into smaller and smaller pieces. They reasoned that if the cutting-up process were continued, a particle that could not be further divided would finally remain. They named this particle "Atom." They believed that each substance had a characteristic atom.

Today we know that there are only about 100 kinds of atoms. These atoms combine to make everything we can see, touch, taste, or smell. But we cannot see individual atoms because they are unbelievably small. For instance, several million billion carbon atoms form the period which ends this sentence.

Atoms are not indivisible but are composed of several parts. Modern scientists picture each one as a miniature solar system with a *nucleus* at its center. *Electrons* spin rapidly around the nucleus in a manner similar to the way the earth and the other planets rotate around the sun. This picture shows how an enlarged lithium atom might appear.

The nucleus is built of two kinds of particles. One kind carries a positive electrical charge (see page 100) which exactly equals the negative charge on an electron. It is called a *proton*. The other kind has no charge; it is electrically neutral. It is called a *neutron*. There are three protons and four neutrons in the nucleus of this lithium atom. Three electrons are whirling around the nucleus.

About 99.95 percent of the weight of the atom is found in its nucleus because electrons weigh only about one two-thousandth as much as protons or neutrons. Even these nuclear particles weigh less than a million-billion-billionth of a pound. But they are so tiny that a cubic inch of them, packed tightly together, would weigh more than a billion tons.

Atoms consist mostly of empty space. For example, if the nucleus of a hydrogen atom were as large as a basketball, its electron would be whirling over a mile away. To put it another way, if all the electrons, protons, and neutrons in your body were packed as tightly together as possible you could hide under a grain of sand.

Photo: courtesy Lithium Corp.

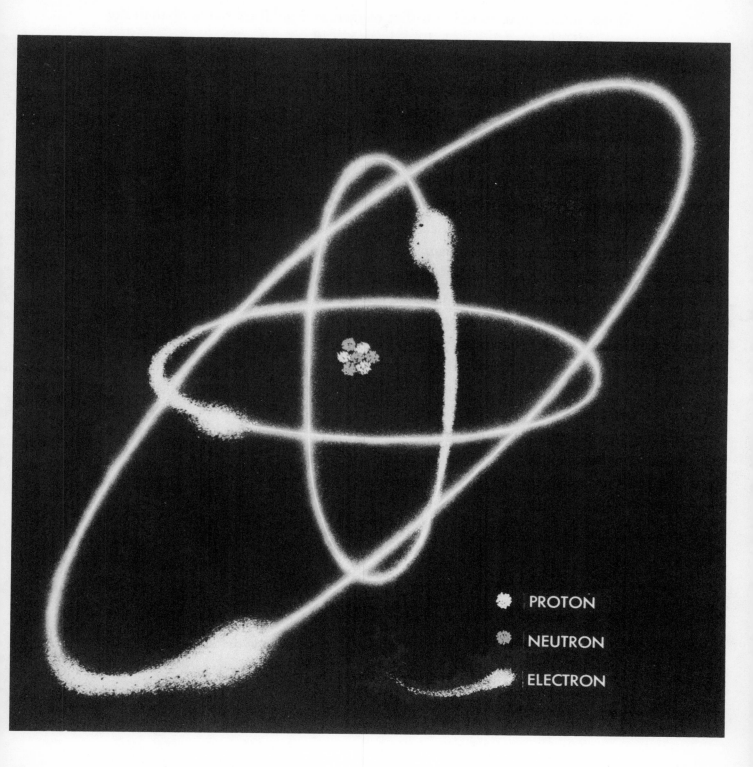

PROTON

NEUTRON

ELECTRON

A HUNDRED KINDS OF ATOMS

IF SOMEONE were to tell you that oxygen and gold are made of the same materials, you might not believe him. Yet, this is true if we compare their atoms. An electron of a gold atom is just like an electron of an oxygen atom —or of any other atom. There is no difference between a proton from an atom of uranium and one from an atom of carbon. Therefore, we can say that atoms differ primarily in the numbers of each kind of particle they contain.

A substance formed of any one kind of atom is known as an *element*. An element cannot be changed into another substance by ordinary chemical methods; nor can an element be made from other substances. Carbon, copper, gold, iron, lead, mercury, silver, sulfur, and tin are elements which were known before the Christian era. The tenth element, arsenic, was not discovered until twelve and one-half centuries after the birth of Christ. Today, we know 101 elements.

The table on the opposite page lists all the elements numerically by their *atomic numbers*. The atomic number of an element indicates the number of protons in the nucleus of its atom, as well as the number of electrons rotating around the nucleus. The table also shows the chemist's abbreviation or symbol for each element, and its atomic weight. The atomic weight of an element is not its weight in ounces or grams. It merely shows the relative weights of the atoms when the atomic weight of oxygen is set equal to 16.

All of the atoms of a given element have the same number of protons in their nuclei and the same number of whirling electrons. But all the atoms of an element are not necessarily alike. Some of the atoms may contain extra neutrons in their nuclei. As a result, the various kinds of atoms of a given element have slightly different weights. These varieties are called *isotopes* of the element. Chemically, isotopes behave in the same manner as normal atoms.

Photo: Ewing Galloway

	Atomic Number	Symbol	Atomic Weight		Atomic Number	Symbol	Atomic Weight
Hydrogen	1	H	1.008	Antimony	51	Sb	121.76
Helium	2	He	4.003	Tellurium	52	Te	127.61
Lithium	3	Li	6.940	Iodine	53	I	126.92
Beryllium	4	Be	9.013	Xenon	54	Xe	131.3
Boron	5	B	10.82	Cesium	55	Cs	132.91
Carbon	6	C	12.010	Barium	56	Ba	137.36
Nitrogen	7	N	14.008	Lanthanum	57	La	138.92
Oxygen	8	O	16.000	Cerium	58	Ce	140.13
Fluorine	9	F	19.00	Praseodymium	59	Pr	140.92
Neon	10	Ne	20.183	Neodymium	60	Nd	144.27
Sodium	11	Na	22.997	Promethium	61	Pm	147.
Magnesium	12	Mg	24.32	Samarium	62	Sm	150.43
Aluminum	13	Al	26.97	Europium	63	Eu	152.0
Silicon	14	Si	28.06	Gadolinium	64	Gd	156.9
Phosphorus	15	P	30.98	Terbium	65	Tb	159.2
Sulfur	16	S	32.066	Dysprosium	66	Dy	162.46
Chlorine	17	Cl	35.457	Holmium	67	Ho	164.94
Argon	18	A	39.944	Erbium	68	Er	167.2
Potassium	19	K	39.096	Thulium	69	Tm	169.4
Calcium	20	Ca	40.08	Ytterbium	70	Yb	173.04
Scandium	21	Sc	45.10	Lutecium	71	Lu	174.99
Titanium	22	Ti	47.90	Hafnium	72	Hf	178.6
Vanadium	23	V	50.95	Tantalum	73	Ta	180.88
Chromium	24	Cr	52.01	Wolfram	74	W	183.92
Manganese	25	Mn	54.93	Rhenium	75	Re	186.31
Iron	26	Fe	55.85	Osmium	76	Os	190.2
Cobalt	27	Co	58.94	Iridium	77	Ir	193.1
Nickel	28	Ni	58.69	Platinum	78	Pt	195.23
Copper	29	Cu	63.54	Gold	79	Au	197.2
Zinc	30	Zn	65.38	Mercury	80	Hg	200.61
Gallium	31	Ga	69.72	Thallium	81	Tl	204.4
Germanium	32	Ge	72.60	Lead	82	Pb	207.21
Arsenic	33	As	74.91	Bismuth	83	Bi	209.00
Selenium	34	Se	78.96	Polonium	84	Po	210.
Bromine	35	Br	79.916	Astatine	85	At	211.
Krypton	36	Kr	83.7	Radon	86	Rn	222.
Rubidium	37	Rb	85.48	Francium	87	Fa	223.0
Strontium	38	Sr	87.63	Radium	88	Ra	226.05
Yttrium	39	Y	88.92	Actinium	89	Ac	227.05
Zirconium	40	Zr	91.22	Thorium	90	Th	232.12
Niobium	41	Nb	92.91	Protactinium	91	Pa	231.
Molybdenum	42	Mo	95.95	Uranium	92	U	238.07
Technetium	43	Tc	99.	Neptunium	93	Np	237.
Ruthenium	44	Ru	101.7	Plutonium	94	Pu	239.
Rhodium	45	Rh	102.91	Americium	95	Am	241.
Palladium	46	Pd	106.7	Curium	96	Cm	242.
Silver	47	Ag	107.880	Berkelium	97	Bk	243.
Cadmium	48	Cd	112.41	Californium	98	Cf	244.
Indium	49	In	114.76	Einsteinium	99	E	247.
Tin	50	Sn	118.70	Fermium	100	Fm	254.
				Mendelevium	101	Mv	256.

UNSTABLE (Neptunium 93 through Mendelevium 101)

MOLECULES

EACH OF MORE than half a million substances has its own distinctive group of atoms. These groups, which are held together by electrical forces, are called *molecules*.

A molecule is the smallest particle of a substance that can exist alone. The molecules of a few gases are composed of a single atom. Other molecules contain millions of atoms. Regardless of the number of atoms they contain, molecules are very small. A glass of water, for example, contains about ten trillion trillion of them.

The electrons of an atom which travel at equal distances from the nucleus are said to occupy the same shell. The shell closest to the nucleus can hold two electrons. The next shell can hold 8 electrons, the third shell 18, the fourth 32, and the fifth 50. But regardless of its capacity, when a shell is the outermost shell of an atom it can hold no more than eight electrons.

The outer shell determines how an atom will behave. If its outer shell is incomplete, the atom is restless. It seeks to add electrons to complete the shell or to lose them so that the last complete shell is exposed. The number of electrons an atom can add or lose is called its *valence*.

When an atom which can lose electrons contacts an atom that can add them, electrons pass from one atom to the other. By losing negatively-charged electrons, the first atom is left with a positive electrical charge. By adding them, the second atom becomes negatively charged. Because opposite charges attract one another, the atoms are electrically bonded to form a molecule.

If we were to picture atoms with an arm for each valence point, we would see that some have no arms. These are one-atom molecules. Some have but one arm, some have two, and others have three or four. Atoms that can accept electrons might be thought of as friends of atoms that can donate electrons, but as strangers to others that accept them. Only friendly atoms will lock arms to form molecules. These cartoons show the composition of some common molecules.

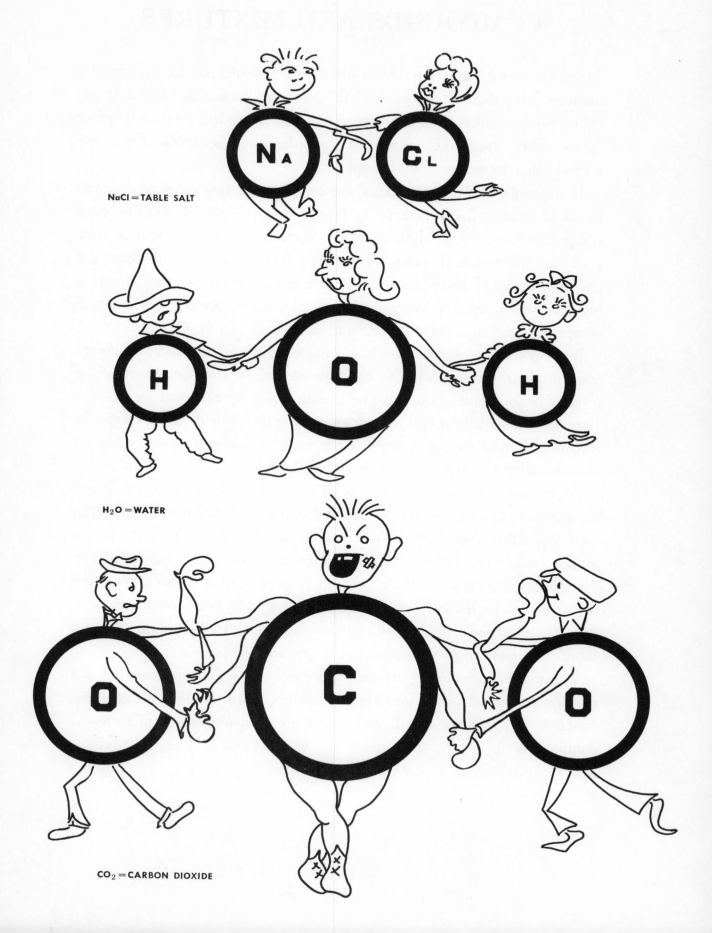

NaCl = TABLE SALT

H_2O = WATER

CO_2 = CARBON DIOXIDE

COMPOUNDS AND MIXTURES

ALTHOUGH THEY MAY NOT be aware of it, these people are breathing a mixture (air), have compounds (salt and water) contained in a mixture (glass) before them, and are eating a mixture (soup) from a mixture (glass) with the aid of a mixture (stainless steel spoons). There are several other mixtures around them.

If the molecules of a substance are composed of two or more different kinds of atoms, the substance is known as a *compound*. Because each compound has its own characteristic molecule, it also has a definite composition. A molecule of water, for example, always has one atom of oxygen and two atoms of hydrogen (H_2O). The composition of water, then, is always two volumes of hydrogen to one of oxygen. Some other common compounds are table salt ($NaCl$) and cane sugar ($C_{12}H_{22}O_{11}$).

The molecules of compounds are the products of chemical reactions. During their formation heat, light, or electricity may be given off or absorbed. Compounds also must be broken down by chemical means. For instance, the hydrogen and oxygen atoms in a molecule of water cannot be separated by pulling them apart. They separate easily, however, when an electric current is passed through the water.

A *mixture* is comprised of two or more compounds or elements. These compounds or elements may be thoroughly intermixed, but each retains its own properties. No chemical reaction occurs during the formation of a mixture to create a characteristic structural unit, such as a molecule. The ingredients of a mixture, therefore, can be present in any proportion. And because their ingredients are not bonded together by chemical forces, mixtures can often be separated by mechanical means. You could easily sort a mixture of licorice sticks, cinnamon drops, and peppermints.

Many substances which we see or use every day are mixtures. Air is a mixture composed almost entirely of elements. Paper, milk, soil, gasoline, concrete, steel, glass, blood, and many other materials are mixtures of compounds.

Photo: Ewing Galloway

CHANGE: PHYSICAL AND CHEMICAL

A PAPER IS TORN; a lump of sugar dissolves and disappears in a cup of coffee; a log is sawed into lumber; water boils, steams, and disappears—in each instance something changes. But in none of these changes does the substance involved lose its identity. A small piece of paper differs only in size from a large piece. If coffee evaporates, the sugar it contains can be recovered. Lumber is made of the same wood that once formed the log. And atmospheric water vapor may condense in small drops on the window pane. A change of this kind, in which the structure of the molecule is not altered, although its position relative to other molecules is altered, is called a physical change.

If the paper is burned, the lump of sugar is charred, the log is burned, or the water is split into hydrogen and oxygen, another type of change takes place. The substance undergoing the change disappears and one or more different substances appear. In this kind of change the molecules of the substance involved are not simply torn apart from one another. Their structures are completely altered. We call this kind of change a chemical change.

Chemical and physical changes are usually well-marked and readily defined. However, many changes which occur in nature, in industry, in the home, and in the laboratory are complicated combinations of both chemical and physical changes which occur simultaneously or nearly so. These combined changes can be analyzed only after careful study.

Photos: Jack McCormick; The Weyerhaeuser Timber Company

FOUR KINDS OF CHEMICAL REACTIONS

IN A CHEMICAL REACTION, such as those which occur in this laboratory, the atoms of the reacting substances are rearranged to form an entirely different substance or substances. These reactions may release heat, light, or electrical energy. In this case, the reaction is said to be *exothermic* (from Greek words meaning "heat" and "out of"). Or, they may absorb energy. These are known as an *endothermic* reaction (from Greek words meaning "heat" and "within"). Or, there may be no apparent change in the energy levels of the substances involved.

There are four main types of chemical reactions:

(1) *Combination.* Two or more elements or simple compounds combine to form a single complex substance.

Example: Iron plus oxygen yields iron oxide (rust).

(2) *Decomposition.* A compound splits into two or more simple compounds or elements. Heat and electricity are the agents most commonly used to decompose substances.

Example: Limestone when heated yields lime and carbon dioxide.

(3) *Replacement.* One element takes the place of another element in a compound.

Example: Aluminum plus iron oxide yields aluminum oxide plus iron.

(4) *Double Replacement.* Two compounds interchange parts to produce two new compounds. Each of the original compounds separates into two parts, called positive and negative ions. The positive ion of one compound joins with the negative ion of the other, and vice versa, forming new compounds.

Example: Silver nitrate plus sodium chloride (table salt) yields silver chloride plus sodium nitrate.

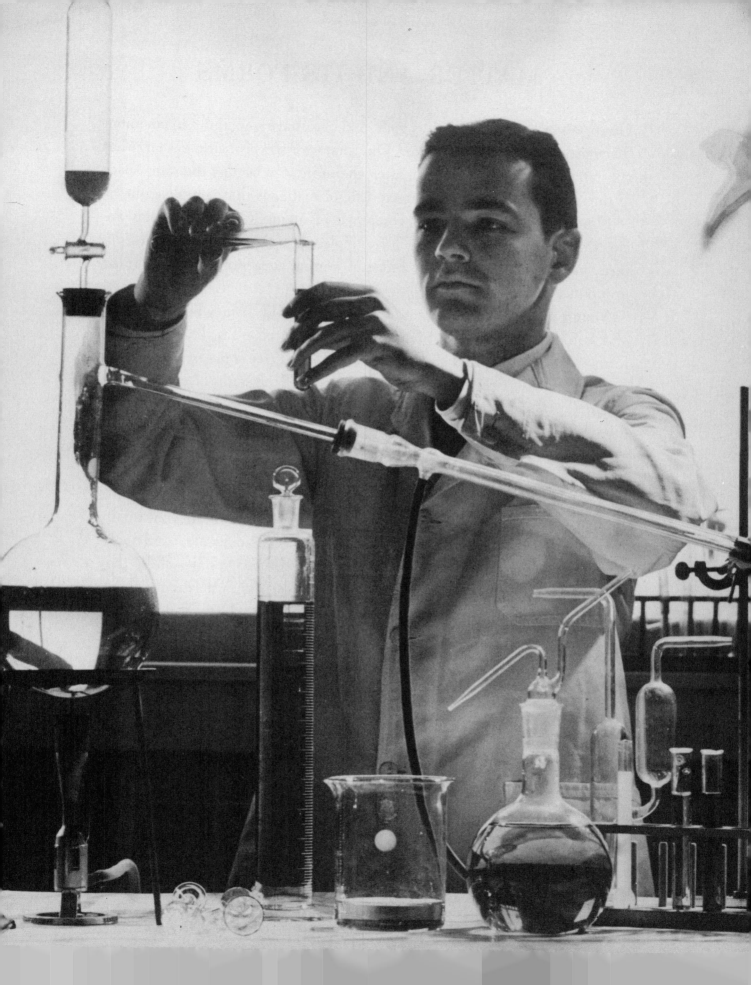

MATTER AND ITS FORMS

GOLD, water, iron, wood, air, paper, and glass have something in common. They are all composed of *matter*. One characteristic of matter is that it has substance. No two portions of matter, therefore, can occupy the same space at the same time. A second characteristic of matter is that it has weight.

Fundamentally, all matter is composed of atoms. Groups of atoms are electrically bonded together to form molecules. And the molecules, in turn, may be held together by forces of mutual attraction, thereby joining to produce visible matter.

Matter may assume the form of a solid, like gold. It may be in the form of a liquid, like water. Or it may be in the form of a gas, like air. These forms—solid, liquid, and gas—are known as the three *states of matter*. You can undoubtedly see several examples of each of the states of matter about you now. If you were at the seashore, you might be standing on a solid (the rock), surrounded by gas (the air), and looking out over a vast expanse of liquid (the ocean).

Even though most matter appears to be static or motionless, the particles which form matter are constantly moving. Electrons are speeding around the nucleus of each atom in a never-ending journey. Atoms are continually varying their positions within the structure of each molecule. And molecules may constantly vibrate in rather fixed positions, as in solids; they may slip and slide one over the other, as in liquids; or they may move about, frequently colliding with one another, only to bound away and collide again, as in gases.

Photo: Werner Stay from F.P.G

GASES

GAS MOLECULES combine the talents of daredevil racers and expert tumblers. At room temperature they travel over a thousand miles per hour. But even a thimbleful of gas contains nearly 200 billion times as many molecules as there are people in the United States. During a single second each gas molecule collides with other molecules as many times as your heart will beat in your entire lifetime.

Under normal conditions, gas molecules are widely spaced. When pressure is applied, however, the molecules are forced together, reducing the volume of the gas. The air in your living room would fit into a suitcase if it were subjected to sufficiently high pressure. In addition, every gas can expand infinitely. Regardless of the size of the container in which a sample of gas is placed, its molecules will scatter until the entire space is occupied uniformly.

Countless speeding gas molecules constantly bombard the walls of their containing vessel, imparting some force with each impact. The sum of these impacts results in a continuous pressure upon the walls. If the gas is compressed, the same number of molecules bombard a smaller area of wall space. The pressure exerted by a gas consequently increases as the gas is compressed. If the gas is heated, its molecules are supplied with additional energy and they strike the walls more often and with greater force. The pressure exerted by a gas increases, therefore, as its temperature rises.

Like other forms of matter, gases have substance. Therefore, air—a gas—can support this parachute and float its passenger gently to the ground. Gases also have weight. But the weight of a gas is considerably less, volume for volume, than that of either a liquid or solid in which the molecules are much more closely packed.

When gases meet, their rapidly bouncing molecules intermingle freely. Because the molecules of a gas are so far apart, the molecules of other gases easily fit into spaces between them. There is no limit to the volume of one gas that can mix or diffuse into another gas.

Photo: Ewing Galloway

LIQUIDS

NATURE HAS FEW LIQUIDS. Water is the only common one. But man has learned to make a variety of new liquids, although he uses none of these in such volume nor for so many purposes as he uses water.

When a substance is changed from a liquid to a gas—as water into steam—the volume of the gas is about 1,650 times greater than that of the liquid. The number and size of the molecules in the gas and liquid, however, are exactly the same. The difference between the two states is that distances between molecules are great in gases, but very small in liquids.

Because their molecules are so close, liquids can be compressed only slightly. A pressure 12,000 times greater than normal reduces the volume of water only 20 percent. Changes of temperature likewise have slight effect on the volume of a liquid when contrasted with effects they produce in a gas.

The nearness of molecules in a liquid allows them to attract one another strongly. Therefore, the molecules stick together. But their mutual attraction is not great enough to prevent them from moving about freely and rapidly, allowing the liquid to flow and assume the shape of its container. If the capacity of the container exceeds the volume of the liquid, the molecules of the liquid do not scatter to fill the space uniformly. They stick together much too tightly to allow that. The liquid, therefore, will have a definite upper surface.

The forces operating on a molecule within a liquid are the same in all directions. But in the surface layer of the liquid the forces are not balanced. Molecules within the liquid tend to pull a molecule of the surface layer into the liquid; other surface molecules tend to pull it sideways. But there are no molecules to pull it upward. This unbalance produces surface tension. The liquid surface behaves like a tightly-stretched elastic film. The strength of this film depends upon the kind of liquid. A steel needle will "float" on water but not on the weaker surface film of alcohol.

Photo: F.P.G.

SOLIDS

A SOLID IS MATTER in its most compact form. Solids are virtually incompressible because their molecules are so tightly packed. And unlike liquids and gases, solids cannot flow. You would not expect this ice to cascade over Niagara Falls as liquid water does. The forces of attraction between the molecules of a solid are so great that they do not tumble and rebound from place to place like those of gases and liquids. Instead, they merely vibrate in more or less fixed positions. This stability of structure causes a solid to maintain a definite shape which is independent of the shape of the container in which it is placed.

There are three general classes of solids. Crystalline solids are the most important. They occur as particles, called crystals, which have a shape that is characteristic for each substance. Each crystal has four or more flat faces which meet in straight edges. Salt, sugar, quartz, and diamonds are a few crystalline solids.

Plastic solids, such as clay, can be deformed permanently by pressure to any desired degree. Vitreous or glassy solids are actually supercooled liquids. They behave as solids at lower temperatures, but when heated they gradually soften rather than melting at a definite temperature. Asphalt, glass, and tar are vitreous solids.

Solids possess several properties not exhibited by matter in other states. *Tenacity* is the ability of a solid to resist forces which tend to pull it apart. *Malleability* is the property which allows some metals, such as gold and tin, to be rolled or hammered into very thin sheets. *Ductility* is the capacity for a substance to be drawn out to form fine wires. Some solids, such as platinum, can be drawn into a wire so thin it can be threaded lengthwise through a human hair. *Hardness* is probably the most familiar property restricted to solids. The degree of hardness is measured by the ability of an object to scratch other substances.

Photo: Bud Barnett

CHANGES OF STATE

DRYING CLOTHES, making ice cubes, melting paraffin—in each of these common activities something disappears and perhaps something else seems to take its place. Matter is changed from one state to another: from liquid to gas, liquid to solid, or solid to liquid.

Heat is absorbed when a solid melts. But this heat does not raise the temperature of the substance. It does serve to overcome the cohesive forces between molecules, allowing them to move more freely and to form a liquid. The absorption of heat by a melting solid is put to use in the cooling of food by ice.

Some of the molecules of a liquid move more rapidly than others. Those which reach the surface with sufficient energy escape from the attractive forces of their neighbors and mix with the molecules of the air, thus the liquid slowly disappears or evaporates. This happens when clothes are hung to dry. Heating imparts greater energy to the molecules of a liquid, allowing many more to break through the surface in a given time. That is why clothes dry faster on warm days.

If sufficient heat is applied to a liquid, its boiling point will be reached. At this temperature the molecules within the liquid, as well as those at its surface, have sufficient energy to escape as a gas or vapor. Bubbles of vapor form throughout the liquid, rise to the surface and burst—an action we call boiling.

Life as we know it is possible because of the temperature of our planet and the heat relations of the substances which compose it. This unique combination results in the coexistence of the three states of matter. If the earth's temperature were slightly higher, all would be gas. If its temperature were lower, all would be solid.

Photo: Ben Mitchell from Black Star

DISPERSIONS

DISPERSIONS consist of particles of one substance scattered more or less evenly through a second substance. There are four general classes of dispersions, based upon the size of the scattered particles. When these particles are of molecular size or less, the particles will not settle out and the dispersion is called a true solution.

In *coarse dispersions,* the particles are visible with the unaided eye. In *fine dispersions,* they can be seen only with a microscope. In *colloidal dispersions,* they are too small to be seen with a microscope, but are larger than single molecules. *True solutions* are dispersions in which the particles are of molecular size or less, and will not settle out.

In a dispersion, the substance that is scattered—such as insect poison sprayed from an airplane—is called the dispersed or inner phase. The other substance, in this example the air, is called the dispersion medium, or outer phase. The following table lists eight kinds of dispersions. The ninth possibility, the dispersion of a gas in a gas, always results in a true solution.

Solutions are mixtures which are homogeneous or exactly the same throughout. The scattered substance (solute), such as sugar, is said to be dissolved in the second substance (the solvent), such as coffee. Even though liquid solutions are the most familiar, there are several other kinds.

Solutions are vital to every living thing on earth. The air around us is a solution of gases. The vast oceans, lakes, and rivers of the earth are liquid solutions. And liquid solutions fill the bodies of all plants and animals.

TYPES OF DISPERSIONS

Dispersion Medium	Dispersed Phase	General Name	Examples
Gas	Liquid	Fog	Insect sprays, clouds, fog
Gas	Solid	Smoke	Smoke
Liquid	Gas	Foam	Whipped cream
Liquid	Liquid	Emulsion	Milk
Liquid	Solid	Suspension	Soapy water, India ink
Solid	Gas		White hair, pumice stone
Solid	Liquid		Jelly, cheese
Solid	Solid		Metal alloys

TYPES OF SOLUTIONS

Solvent	Solute	Examples	Solvent	Solute	Examples
Liquid	Gas	Carbonated water	Solid	Gas	Hydrogen in platinum
Liquid	Liquid	Rubbing alcohol	Solid	Liquid	Mercury in copper
Liquid	Solid	Sugar in coffee	Solid	Solid	Gold in lead

Photos: Sugar Inf. Inc.; American Forest Products Industries

DENSITY AND SPECIFIC GRAVITY

ALL MATTER HAS WEIGHT. But from experience we know that some kinds of matter are heavier than others. A piece of iron, for instance, is much heavier than a similar piece of aluminum. But a large piece of aluminum may weigh as much as, or more than a smaller piece of iron. So, to compare the weights of different objects (especially if they differ greatly in size) their weights must be given in terms of portions of equal size.

Density is an expression of the weights of various substances expressed in identical units of volume. The density of this large chunk of plastic foam is obviously much smaller than the density of the meringue pie it is balancing.

To determine the density of a substance, its weight is divided by its volume. The density of iron is found to be 490 pounds per cubic foot in English measure, or 7.9 grams per cubic centimeter in metric measure. The density of aluminum is 170 pounds per cubic foot, or 2.7 grams per cubic centimeter. (See page 114.)

Specific gravity is a handy measure of the relative densities of various substances. It is obtained by dividing the density of a substance by that of water. In metric terms, the density of water is one gram per cubic centimeter. If the metric system of measure is employed, no redetermination is necessary because a quantity is not changed when it is divided by one. Therefore, the specific gravity of a substance is numerically equal to its density expressed in grams per cubic centimeter.

DENSITY AND SPECIFIC GRAVITY OF SOME COMMON SUBSTANCES

	Pounds/ Cubic Foot	Grams/Cubic Centimeter and Specific Gravity		Pounds/ Cubic Foot	Grams/Cubic Centimeter and Specific Gravity
Pine Wood......	30	0.5	Aluminum	168	2.7
Ice.............	57	0.9	Iron............	493	7.9
Water..........	62.4	1.0	Gold	1206	19.3

Photo: courtesy Westinghouse

THINGS THAT FLOAT

ARCHIMEDES, a mathematician who lived 22 centuries ago, discovered the secret of things that float. *The buoyant force exerted by a fluid on any object is equal to the weight of fluid that the object displaces.* If the buoyant force is greater than the weight of the object, the object will float. Even if an object sinks, its apparent weight will be reduced by an amount equal to the weight of the fluid it displaces. This is why a rock seems to weigh less in water than it does in the air.

When the specific gravity of an object is less than the specific gravity of the fluid in which it is immersed, the object will displace a volume of fluid with a weight greater than its own. The object, therefore, will float.

The specific gravity of iron is 7.9, so solid iron will not float in water (specific gravity = 1). But if a piece of iron is flattened and shaped into a hollow vessel which will displace a weight of water greater than its own, the iron will float. This principle is employed by huge ocean liners, such as the S.S. *United States* shown here in New York harbor.

Steel-framed airships, such as this Navy blimp, and heavy fabric and rubber balloons that float in the air operate on the same principle. Because they are filled with helium or some other gas that has a specific gravity smaller than that of air, the gas-filled bags displace a volume of air with a greater weight than their own. Therefore, they float.

A submarine is able to sink or float by varying its specific gravity. Basically, a submarine is a hollow steel cylinder with compartments which can be filled with water or air as desired. When they are filled with air, the ship is light enough to float. When the compartments are water-filled, however, the specific gravity of the ship is greater than that of water, and the submarine sinks.

Photos: courtesy U. S. Lines Co.; Goodyear Aircraft Corp.

ACIDS AND BASES

AN ACID is formed if the molecules of a hydrogen compound break up into negatively and positively-charged particles (ions) when the compound is dissolved in water. Acids share several characteristics: 1) They contain hydrogen ions; 2) they taste sour; 3) they conduct electricity; 4) when magnesium, aluminum, manganese, zinc, chromium, iron, nickel, tin, or lead is placed in an acid solution, the metal replaces the hydrogen in the acid, liberating hydrogen gas.

Most people believe that an acid is a liquid that will make holes in their clothing, cause agonizing pain if accidentally dropped on their skin, and cause almost instantaneous death if swallowed. Sulfuric acid (H_2SO_4), hydrochloric acid (HCl), and nitric acid (HNO_3), the acids most often used in the chemical laboratory and in industry, live up to these dire standards. But boric acid (H_2BO_3) is used as a soothing eye wash. Vinegar, a weak solution of acetic acid (CH_3COOH), is used in cooking. Carbonic acid (H_2CO_3) produces the soda water from which soft drinks are made. Ascorbic acid ($C_6H_8O_{16}$), better known as Vitamin C, is an important part of our daily diet.

Bases or hydroxides are another important class of chemicals. They are formed by compounds whose molecules break up into negatively-charged hydroxyl ions, composed of oxygen and hydrogen, and some positive ion. Bases have a bitter taste and a slippery, or soapy feel. Like those of acids, solutions of hydroxides conduct electricity. One of these laboratory bottles contains ammonium hydroxide (NH_4OH), a common base.

When an acid and a base are mixed, a double replacement reaction occurs. One product is a compound formed by the negative ion of the acid and the positive ion of the base. It is known as a salt. The second product is always pure water (H_2O). One of the most common reactions of this type occurs when a farmer puts lime on an acid soil. The lime combines with water in the soil to form a base which then reacts with the soil acids.

Photo: courtesy Allied Chemical and Dye Corp.

MATTER IN MOTION: THE FIRST LAW

THREE LAWS OF MOTION which govern all matter were formulated by Sir Isaac Newton, an English mathematician. They were contained in his monumental book, *Principia,* or *Principles of Natural Philosophy,* published in 1687. These laws have become the foundation of the modern science of mechanics.

Newton's first law of motion states that *a body at rest tends to remain at rest and a body in motion tends to remain in motion in a straight line and at a constant speed.* The characteristic of matter that causes it to resist change in motion is called inertia. Inertia is a function of the quantity of matter present in an object, the *mass* of the object. A gallon of water has the same mass as the 1,650 gallons of steam into which it can change, because both contain exactly the same number of molecules.

A non-living object cannot begin to move of its own accord. An unbalanced outside force must act upon the object to overcome its inertia. The force must be unbalanced. Two equal forces acting from opposite directions will balance one another and produce no motion.

Moving bodies are retarded by the force of friction (see page 154). In reality, therefore, a force equal and opposite to that of friction must be applied to keep a body moving at a constant speed. In our automobiles, a gas engine supplies this force. To oppose the inertia of a moving automobile and bring it to a quick stop, we apply the brakes.

Two equal forces act between a body moving in a circular path and a second body. One, called centripetal force, acts inwardly to hold the moving body in its path. When you twirl an object on a string, the pull you exert through the string is the centripetal force. The other force, which results from the tendency of inertia to cause the moving body to seek a straight-line course, is centrifugal force. It causes water to fly off of a dog's back when he shakes, or out of clothes when they are whirled in a spin-drier attached to a washing machine. It is the force which thrills you on many whirling carnival rides.

Photo: Ewing Galloway

MATTER IN MOTION: THE SECOND LAW

Sir isaac newton's first law of motion describes what happens when no outside force acts upon a body. His second law describes what happens when such a force is applied. It states that *when an unbalanced force acts upon a body it will change the velocity of the body in the direction of the force.* The change of velocity will be directly proportional to the size of the force and to the time during which it acts on the body, and inversely proportional to the mass of the body.

A small force, thus, will not produce as great a change in the velocity of a body as a large force. And a force will produce a greater change in velocity if it acts on the body for a longer time. But the effect of a force acting upon a body is halved if the mass of the body is doubled.

The explosion of gunpowder lasts but a split second but it can accelerate a bullet from rest or zero miles per hour, to more than 400 miles per hour. An arrow may attain a speed very close to that of a bullet. Its speed, however, is the result of a much smaller force—the recoil of the bowstring—acting for a longer time. When a baseball player "follows through" on his swing, keeping his bat in contact with the ball for as long as possible, he makes use of this principle. By extending the length of time the force of his bat acts on the ball, he may stretch a two-base hit into a home-run.

Photo: H. Armstrong Roberts

MATTER IN MOTION: THE THIRD LAW

NEWTON'S THIRD LAW of motion is a very simple statement that describes an occurrence associated with every application of force: *for every action there is an equal and opposite reaction.*

When a gun or cannon is fired, a force released by the explosion of a charge of powder causes a shell to accelerate very rapidly forward. An equal force is directed against the gun and causes it to accelerate backwards. We say that the gun "kicks" or recoils. The gun, of course, does not accelerate as rapidly nor travel as far as the shell because the force must act upon a much greater mass.

Some other examples of actions and reactions are given below.

ACTION	REACTION
Man jumps from rowboat to dock	Rowboat lurches away from dock
Stretch rubber band between thumbs, pull with left thumb	Must also pull with right thumb to stretch band
Water squirts out of garden sprinkler	Garden sprinkler turns
Man paddling canoe pushes backward against water	Canoe moves forward

Photo: Official U.S. Navy Photo from Ewing Galloway

HOW WE RECOGNIZE THINGS

WHAT COULD YOU TELL about an elephant from a single touch? You might determine if the elephant were solid, liquid, or gas; firm or soft; smooth, rough, or hairy; moist or dry; warm or cold. By reaching as high as you could to touch it, you would know something of the height of an elephant. And you might smell the elephant while touching it. All the things you would learn are characteristic of the elephant you touched, and of every other elephant in the world.

An elephant always looks like an elephant. It never appears in any other form. But compounds and elements and the substances which they comprise can appear in a variety of forms. Glass, for instance, can be found in the form of a bottle, mirror, statue, window pane, drinking glass, door knob, television tube, vase, or other object. Each of the hundreds of thousands of substances in our world, however, has certain characteristics, called specific properties, by which it can be identified and described. These properties describe the substance regardless of the form in which it may appear.

In the column below the most important specific properties of substances are listed.

SOME SPECIFIC PROPERTIES OF A SUBSTANCE

Physical state—At room temperature is it solid, liquid, or gas?

Color—What color is it?

Odor—Does it have an odor?

Taste—Does it have any taste?

Solubility—Does it dissolve in water or some other solvent?

Hardness—If it is a solid, what substances will it scratch? Which will scratch it?

Elasticity—Is it brittle, inelastic, or flexible?

Boiling point — At what temperature will it change from a liquid to a gas?

Melting point — At what temperature will it change from a solid to a liquid?

Inflammability—Does it burn easily?

Magnetism—Is it attracted by a magnet?

Density—What is its wt. per unit of volume?

Compressibility—What volume changes occur when the substance is subjected to increased pressure?

Electrical conductivity — How easily will an electric current pass through it?

Viscosity—If it is a liquid, does it pour easily?

Thermal expansion — How much does it expand when heated?

Photo: A. W. Blakesley from F.P.G.

CHAPTER II

A WORLD OF LIFE

THE BODIES of all living things—plants, animals, people—are made mostly of a few of the elements: carbon, nitrogen, oxygen, and hydrogen. All living things depend on a few compounds, such as water, proteins, carbohydrates, and vitamins to sustain life. Another compound (chlorophyll, the green substance found in plants) is the major link between the worlds of living and non-living things.

In this chapter you will learn about the basic composition of living things. Plants and animals are made up of non-living substances, upon which they continually depend to remain alive. Yet, each living thing is more than the sum of these substances; each carries *life,* a force which permits it to grow, to get food, to release wastes, and to reproduce its own kind.

Photo: New York Zoological Society

THE ELEMENTS WE BREATHE

WE LIVE at the bottom of a deep sea of gases which we call the atmosphere, or simply the air. The atmosphere is not a compound, nor is it an element. It is a solution of gases, a mixture comprised primarily of elements.

TYPICAL COMPOSITION OF DRY AIR AT SEA LEVEL

Constituent	Percentage of Volume
Nitrogen	78.03
Oxygen	20.99
Argon	0.93
Carbon dioxide	0.04
Hydrogen	0.01
Neon	0.001
Helium	0.0004
Krypton	0.00005
Xenon	0.000006
Radon	0.000001

Two other common components of the air—water vapor and dust—are present in amounts which vary widely from place to place.

The sea of air has been calculated to be as much as 2,000 miles deep. At sea level the column of air which rests on each square foot of the earth weighs more than a ton. At the summit of Mt. Everest, 29,141 feet above sea level, the column of air over each square foot weighs slightly more than five pounds.

Because of the tremendous weight pressing down upon it, the air is highly compressed, and therefore most dense near the ground. As we rise higher above the surface of the earth, the air is under less pressure and becomes less dense.

Photo: Ewing Galloway

ELEMENTS UNDER FOOT

THE EARTH is a storehouse which contains at least some of every stable element. Plants tap the supplies in the earth's crust for necessary raw materials from which they manufacture food for themselves and for all animal life. Man has learned that he, too, can draw on this natural storehouse for his industrial needs. Mines, pits and oil wells are the most common means by which he withdraws supplies directly.

The most abundant mineral compound, silicon dioxide, comprises more than half of the earth's crust. In its pure state, silicon dioxide is known as quartz. Its less pure form is called sand. The ten most common compounds in the earth's crust are shown in the table below.

THE TEN MOST COMMON CHEMICALS IN THE EARTH'S CRUST

Compound	Percentage of the Earth's Crust
Silicon dioxide (SiO_2)	55.2%
Aluminum trioxide (Al_2O_3)	15.3
Calcium oxide (CaO)	8.8
Ferric oxide (FeO)	5.8
Magnesium oxide (MgO)	5.2
Sodium oxide (Na_2O)	2.9
Ferrous oxide (Fe_2O_3)	2.8
Potassium oxide (K_2O)	1.9
Titanium dioxide (TiO_2)	1.6
Phosphorus pentoxide (P_2O_5)	0.3

Photo: Ewing Galloway

OCEANS OF ELEMENTS

Ocean water, the most abundant solution in the world, covers about five-sevenths of the surface of the earth. Each 100-pound measure of this water contains about 3.5 pounds of dissolved chemicals.

The most plentiful of the chemicals dissolved in ocean water is sodium chloride, our common table salt. All the salts in the ocean, if dried and piled together, would cover the entire United States about two feet deep. These compounds are primarily responsible for the salty taste of the water.

At least a small quantity of almost every other element is also found in the sea. The elements most abundantly dissolved in sea water are:

Element	Tons per Cubic Mile of Sea Water
Chlorine	90,000,000
Sodium	53,000,000
Magnesium	5,700,000
Sulfur	4,300,000
Potassium	3,300,000
Calcium	2,400,000
Bromine	310,000
Iodine	200

Photo: courtesy Hawaii Press Bureau

CARBON

CARBON is the most amazing element. Although it forms but 0.03 percent of the crust of the earth, carbon is a constituent of more than 300,000 different substances—ten times the number of all other compounds.

Carbon is able to form such a tremendous variety of compounds because its atoms are extremely sociable. Each carbon atom has four valence "arms" with which it can combine with other atoms. These may be the atoms of other elements. But carbon atoms have the unique ability to link with other carbon atoms, forming rings and long chains.

Pure carbon appears in two crystalline forms and an amorphous, or structureless, condition. One of carbon's crystalline forms is uniform in structure in all directions. In this form, carbon is colorless, transparent, insoluble in all common solvents, a non-conductor of electricity, and it is the hardest of all known substances. We call it a diamond.

Its other crystalline form is known as graphite. In this form, carbon is black, opaque, very soft, greasy to the touch, a conductor of electricity, and is insoluble in the common solvents. The "lead" in your pencil is a mixture of graphite and clay.

Charcoal, peat, coke, lamp black, and the various grades of coal are more or less pure forms of amorphous carbon. These substances differ from the crystalline forms of carbon in that their atoms do not appear to have an organized arrangement.

Carbon is our most useful element because of the many forms in which it occurs. As coal, coke, charcoal, and (in combination with hydrogen) petroleum, it is the most important source of energy to power our machines and to heat our buildings. Even more important, carbon forms a considerable portion of all plants and animals. In fact, about 18 percent of you is carbon. Because carbon compounds were once believed to be produced only by living organisms, they are called organic compounds. The chemistry of carbon compounds is still known as organic chemistry.

Photo: Ewing Galloway

THE CARBON CYCLE

CARBON is the most basic constituent of living matter and of many other natural substances. But the supply of carbon is very limited. In nature, therefore, carbon atoms must be circulated in a manner similar to the way in which we circulate money. Just as a single dollar bill may be used by many people, a single carbon atom may be a part of a lump of coal at one time, part of a molecule of carbon dioxide gas at another time, and at still another time, a part of your own body. This circulation of carbon atoms is called the carbon cycle.

Carbon dioxide is a colorless, odorless gas that comprises about one-thirtieth of the volume of the air. Just as a bank is the main agency for the circulation of money, carbon dioxide in the atmosphere is the main agency for the circulation of carbon.

Green plants continually withdraw carbon dioxide from the atmospheric bank. By combining it with hydrogen, plants manufacture simple sugars. If these sugars are used to supply energy to the plant, carbon dioxide is a by-product of this energy-producing reaction. Or the sugars may be converted into new plant tissue. Thus the carbon is stored in the tissues of a plant and is returned to the atmosphere when the plant burns or decays.

Of course, the plant may be eaten by an animal. In this case, the tissue may be oxidized (see page 64) to supply energy to the animal. The animal exhales carbon dioxide as a by-product. Animals (including people) depend upon plants to supply all the carbon needed to build their bodies. Carbon in animal tissue is circulated when one animal is eaten by another, or when an animal dies and its tissues decay. Decay is another form of oxidation which releases carbon dioxide.

The complete carbon cycle is even more complicated. It includes carbon in the form of limestone and coral, peat and coal, volcanic gases, and petroleum. Regardless of the form in which an atom of carbon may be found, it will eventually be returned to the atmospheric bank. Once returned to the bank, it is ready to begin its circulation once again.

Photos: N. Y. Times; Ewing Galloway; Monkmeyer;
Hawaii Press Bureau; Standard Oil Co. (N. J.)

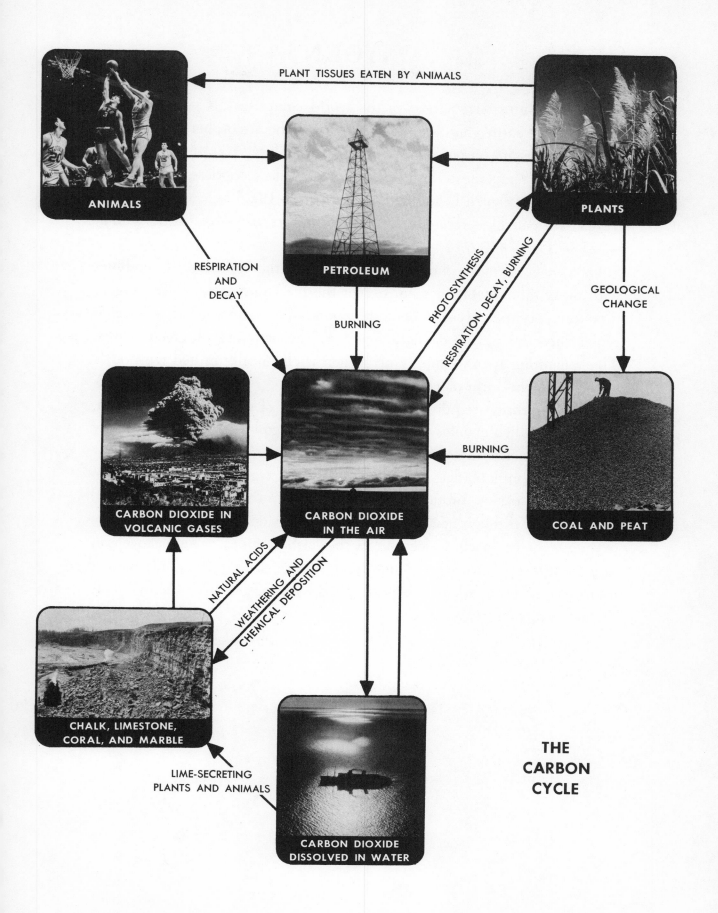

PLANT TISSUES EATEN BY ANIMALS

ANIMALS

PLANTS

PETROLEUM

RESPIRATION AND DECAY

PHOTOSYNTHESIS

RESPIRATION, DECAY, BURNING

GEOLOGICAL CHANGE

BURNING

CARBON DIOXIDE IN VOLCANIC GASES

CARBON DIOXIDE IN THE AIR

BURNING

COAL AND PEAT

NATURAL ACIDS

WEATHERING AND CHEMICAL DEPOSITION

CHALK, LIMESTONE, CORAL, AND MARBLE

LIME-SECRETING PLANTS AND ANIMALS

CARBON DIOXIDE DISSOLVED IN WATER

THE CARBON CYCLE

OXYGEN

THE MOST ABUNDANT THING in the world comprises 50 percent of the weight of the earth's hard crust, 25 percent of the atmosphere, 80 percent of the oceans, and 65 percent of you. We call it oxygen.

At normal temperatures, pure oxygen is a tasteless, odorless, colorless gas. But when it is cooled below its boiling point, $-182.5°$ C. $(-360.5°$ F.), oxygen is a pale blue, strongly magnetic liquid. It turns to a brittle solid at $-227.0°$ C. $(-440.6°$ F.).

Oxygen is the most chemically active of all the elements. It combines with every other stable element except the inert rare gases. Pure oxygen, therefore, occurs only in the atmosphere. The atmospheric supply is replenished during the daylight hours by the activities of green plants. The remaining natural supply of oxygen is chemically united with other elements in the form of various compounds.

All living things require a continuous supply of oxygen for respiration, the process which enables you to derive energy from your food. To allow your body to carry on its life functions, you breathe in enough air each day to fill 13,000 milk bottles. About 500 quarts of oxygen are subtracted from this air as it passes through your lungs, used in oxidation processes, and later released through your lungs as carbon dioxide. When men go where oxygen is scarce (such as deep below the earth in mines, or high above it in airplanes) they must carry a supply of the gas with them. This man is wearing a safety mask which is supplied with oxygen from the cylinders that are strapped to his chest.

Photo: Chemical and Engineering News

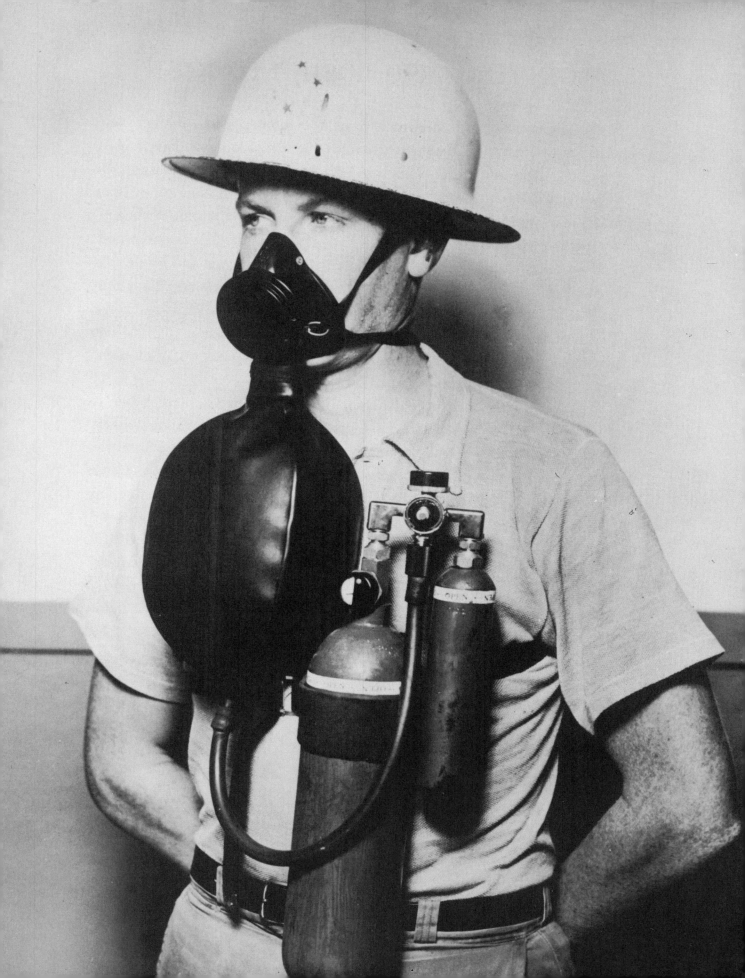

GETTING AND LOSING OXYGEN

A CHEMICAL REACTION in which oxygen combines with another substance is termed an oxidation reaction. Rapid oxidation reactions release noticeable heat and light. They are usually described as combustion, or burning. This roaring fire in the pine forests of southern New Jersey is an example of rapid oxidation. When trees burn, oxygen combines with compounds of carbon, hydrogen, and oxygen present in the leaves and wood. The products of this reaction are primarily carbon dioxide and water.

Slow oxidation reactions are less spectacular than rapid ones. They produce no light, but release an amount of heat equal to that of rapid reactions. The heat is released over such a long period of time that it is often not noticeable. The rusting of iron, drying of oil paints, and decay of plant and animal remains are slow oxidation reactions.

Reduction is the reverse of oxidation. In a reduction reaction, oxygen is removed from, rather than added to a substance. Reduction is brought about by mixing a substance with a chemical which has a stronger attraction for oxygen, known as a reducing agent. During the reaction, oxygen is transferred from the substance to this reducing agent. Therefore, every reduction reaction is accompanied by an oxidation reaction. Reduction reactions are especially important in refining ores to obtain pure metals (see page 190).

The term oxidation is now applied to any chemical reaction in which a substance loses electrons and thereby increases its valence (see page 16). The term reduction is applied to a reaction in which a substance gains electrons and decreases its valence.

Photo: courtesy Aero Service Corp.

HYDROGEN

ITS ATOM is the simplest possible—one electron whirling around a single proton. By virtue of this simple construction, hydrogen has the smallest mass of all substances; consequently, it is the lightest thing in the world. It weighs only one-fourteenth as much as the air you breathe.

Because it is so light, hydrogen has long been used in balloons and other lighter-than-air craft. It was once thought that giant dirigibles—as long as 10 football fields, and weighing more than 20 elephants—would serve as luxury liners of the air. But, hydrogen and oxygen form a highly explosive mixture. On May 6, 1937 the giant German dirigible, *Hindenburg,* burst into flames and crashed at Lakehurst, New Jersey. This accident, pictured here, marked the end of an era.

Hydrogen is still used for weather balloons. Helium, a heavier but non-inflammable rare gas, has supplanted hydrogen in large, lighter-than-air passenger craft. But the short supply of helium and the development of larger and speedier airplanes have made helium-filled aircraft a rarity.

Astronomers believe that free hydrogen comprises a significant portion of the sun and other stars, and it probably exists throughout space between celestial bodies. In fact, hydrogen seems to be the most abundant thing in the universe.

In our atmosphere, hydrogen occurs in a free, gaseous state in infinitely small amounts. In a combined form it is found in all plant and animal tissue, and in petroleum and natural gas. It makes up 11 percent of water by weight, and is a vital component of all acids.

Hydrogen is relatively inactive. A mixture of hydrogen and oxygen, however, combines with a violent explosion when ignited, producing ordinary water (H_2O). Because it combines so readily with oxygen, hydrogen is used as a reducing agent in many industrial refining processes.

Photo: International News

WATER

WATER is the most common of all chemical compounds. It covers about three-fourths of the earth's surface, occurs in vast quantities in the air, and makes up a considerable portion of every plant and animal.

Under ordinary conditions, water is a clear, colorless, odorless liquid. In deep layers, as in oceans and lakes, water may appear to be bluish-green. When cooled to 0° C. (32° F.), water changes into a colorless solid called ice. When heated to 100° C. (212° F.), it boils and changes into a vapor called steam.

Life would be impossible without water. It makes up a large part of the protoplasm of all living things. In your own body, virtually every reaction occurs only when the reacting substances are dissolved in water. For instance, in your stomach digestion takes place only in a water medium. The digested food and the undigested wastes are all carried away in solution. Animals obtain water directly by drinking it, just as these horses are doing, and in the food they eat.

Green plants obtain their supplies of hydrogen and oxygen primarily from water which they absorb through their roots. The hydrogen is used in photosynthesis to produce simple sugars while the oxygen may be freed or used in respiration. And, just as in your body, water is important to the plant as a medium for transportation of food and raw materials. Plants lose a great quantity of water to the air by evaporation from their leaves and stems.

Photo: Allen from Ewing Galloway

THE WATER CYCLE

WATER is a restless wanderer. It seems to be always in a hurry to get somewhere, but stays nowhere for very long.

Water vapor is lighter than air and therefore rises in the atmosphere. As it rises, however, it cools and finally condenses into fine droplets. These droplets, which we see as mist or clouds, coalesce and fall as rain or snow.

Part of the rain or snow evaporates back into the air before it reaches the earth. Another portion runs over the surface of the ground and into streams or lakes. Still another portion seeps into the soil.

Some of the water which enters the soil reappears in springs and rivers. Some flows underground to the ocean. And some either evaporates directly or is absorbed by vegetation and then evaporated from the plants.

Water that reaches a stream or pond may evaporate into the air or it may flow to the ocean, the earth's greatest water reservoir. The oceans contain more than 85 percent of all the earth's water. Vast quantities of water vapor are lost from their surfaces each day.

Ultimately, all the water that enters the air again falls to the earth. But it is continually replaced by new supplies. The circulation of water in nature is called the water cycle.

Photo: Burton Holmes from Ewing Galloway

THE NITROGEN CYCLE

N COMPRISES more than three-fourths of the air. N extends high above the earth and rests upon every acre with a weight of 300 million pounds. You are completely surrounded by N; and N is present in every cell and in every drop of blood in your body.

N, of course, is the chemical symbol for the element nitrogen. Pure nitrogen is an odorless, colorless gas which neither burns nor supports combustion. It liquefies at $-196°$ C. $(321°$ F.$)$ and freezes to a white solid at $-210°$ C. $(-346°$ F.$)$. Although nitrogen is relatively inert, it occurs in a pure state, under natural conditions, only in the atmosphere.

Nitrogen is essential to all living things. Its atoms join with those of carbon, hydrogen, and oxygen and at times with those of sulfur and phosphorus, to form complex protein molecules. Proteins are the basic components of protoplasm, the substance contained in all living cells. Some familiar proteins are the white of an egg, the venom of a poisonous snake, and gamma globulin, a blood derivative now widely used to protect people from polio and other diseases.

Even though every plant and animal requires a continuous supply of nitrogen, only a few simple plants (mostly bacteria) can use uncombined nitrogen. These bacteria live in the soil, or in swellings or tubercles on the roots of green plants. They can combine nitrogen into simple protein compounds, in which form the nitrogen can be absorbed by green plants. Animals obtain their nitrogen by eating plant tissues.

When an animal or plant dies, other kinds of bacteria break down the complex protein molecules in its remains, leaving the nitrogen combined with hydrogen in simple ammonia molecules. Some ammonium compounds can be used immediately by higher plants. Others are oxidized later by soil bacteria into the form of nitrates which can be used by all higher plants.

Each year, throughout the world, many millions of tons of nitrogen are removed from the atmosphere. But the atmospheric supply is not diminished, because a like amount is returned to the air by burning and decay of plant and animal remains. This entire process by which nitrogen is circulated in nature is called the nitrogen cycle.

Photos: Hawaii Press Bureau; Black Star; Ewing Galloway

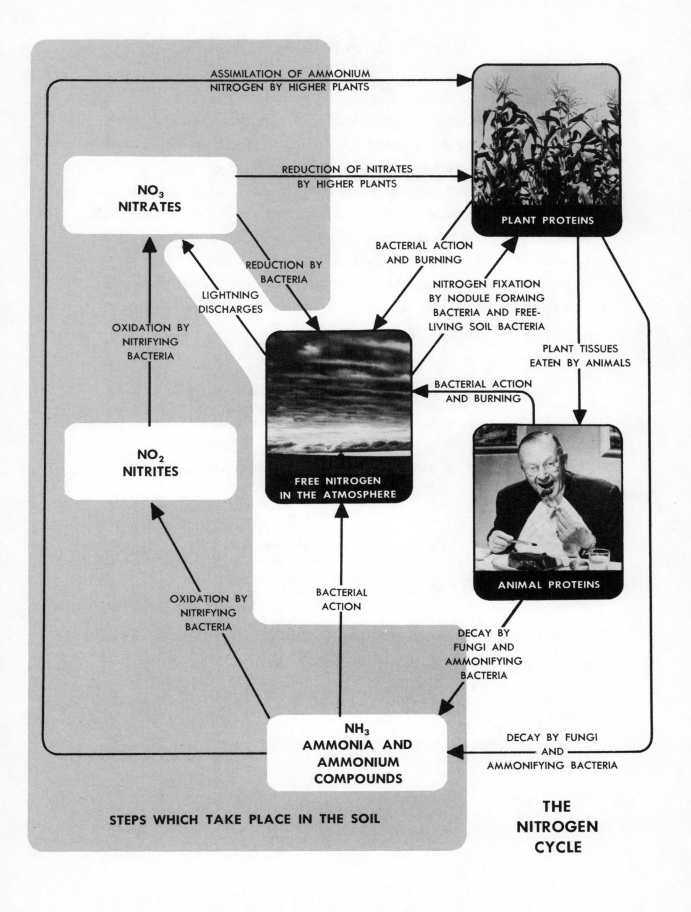

ASSIMILATION OF AMMONIUM
NITROGEN BY HIGHER PLANTS

REDUCTION OF NITRATES
BY HIGHER PLANTS

NO₃
NITRATES

PLANT PROTEINS

BACTERIAL ACTION
AND BURNING

REDUCTION BY
BACTERIA

NITROGEN FIXATION
BY NODULE FORMING
BACTERIA AND FREE-
LIVING SOIL BACTERIA

LIGHTNING
DISCHARGES

OXIDATION BY
NITRIFYING
BACTERIA

PLANT TISSUES
EATEN BY ANIMALS

BACTERIAL ACTION
AND BURNING

NO₂
NITRITES

FREE NITROGEN
IN THE ATMOSPHERE

ANIMAL PROTEINS

OXIDATION BY
NITRIFYING
BACTERIA

BACTERIAL
ACTION

DECAY BY
FUNGI AND
AMMONIFYING
BACTERIA

NH₃
AMMONIA AND
AMMONIUM
COMPOUNDS

DECAY BY FUNGI
AND
AMMONIFYING BACTERIA

STEPS WHICH TAKE PLACE IN THE SOIL

THE
NITROGEN
CYCLE

WHAT MAKES A MAN?

Enough fat to make seven bars of soap; enough iron to make a medium-sized nail; enough potassium to make a shotgun shell; enough magnesium for a dose of magnesia; enough sugar to sweeten a gallon of lemonade; enough lime to whitewash your backyard fence; enough sulfur to give your dog a flea bath; enough phosphorus to make 2,200 match heads; and enough water to wash the dishes after three meals—these are needed to make the body of an average-sized man. Sold as raw materials, the components of your body would be worth about a dollar.

In a complete analysis, the human body has been found to be composed of twenty elements. The following table enumerates these elements.

COMPOSITION OF THE HUMAN BODY

Element	Percentage	Place of Occurrence in Body
Oxygen	65.00%	water, carbohydrates, proteins, fats
Carbon	18.00	carbohydrates, proteins, fats
Hydrogen	10.00	water, carbohydrates, proteins, fats, stomach acids
Nitrogen	3.00	proteins
Calcium	2.00	bones, teeth, blood
Phosphorus	1.00	bones, teeth, muscles, nerves, brain
Potassium	0.35	soft tissues, milky secretions
Sulfur	0.25	proteins
Sodium	0.15	common salt
Chlorine	0.15	common salt, stomach acids
Magnesium	0.05	bones, soft tissues, body fluids
Iron	0.004	red blood cells, muscles, liver, kidneys, spleen
Manganese	0.003	?
Fluorine	Trace	teeth, bones
Silicon	Trace	?
Iodine	Trace	thyroid secretions
Copper	Trace	muscles, bones, liver, blood, aids in utilization of iron
Cobalt	Trace	?
Zinc	Trace	?
Bromine	Trace	?
Aluminum	Trace	?
Selenium	Trace	?
Boron	Trace	?

Photo: courtesy New York Times

FOOD FOR MAN

THIS GIRL is going to eat all of the meat that is piled in a miniature mountain behind her. She, as well as each of us, will consume this tremendous amount of meat during a lifetime.

Dr. Norman J. Berrill of McGill University* estimates that an average person in a lifetime of 70 years will consume a total of about 40 tons of food. This will include:

    33,600 pounds of vegetables, fruits, nuts, and berries
    13,300 pounds of grain in the form of bread and cereals
    11,900 pounds of meat, fish, and poultry
     9,100 pounds of potatoes
     7,700 pounds of sugar
     4,500 pounds of fats and oils
     1,400 pounds of tea, chocolate, and coffee
    25,200 eggs
    17,500 quarts of milk

In addition to water, salts, and vitamins (none of which furnish nourishment for the body) foodstuffs are composed of several chemical classes of foods. *Carbohydrates,* which comprise about 70 percent of our diet, are our chief source of energy. In their molecules, carbon is combined with hydrogen and oxygen which are present in the same ratio as they occur in water (H_2O). *Fats* are a more concentrated, but less abundant source of energy. They comprise slightly less than 30 percent of our diet. Fats are also composed only of carbon, hydrogen, and oxygen. In these compounds, however, hydrogen and oxygen do not occur in the same ratio as in water. *Proteins* are complex compounds of carbon, hydrogen, oxygen, and nitrogen, and sometimes sulfur and phosphorus. Proteins furnish the body with materials for growth and repair.

*Norman J. Berrill, "How Long Can the Earth Keep Us Eating?" *MacLean's Magazine,* 68:16-20, June 11, 1955.

Photo: Ken Bell Photography Ltd.

WHAT MAKES A PLANT?

A PLANT is mostly water. A cucumber, for instance, is about 96 percent water and a corn plant is 80 percent water. The remaining portion of the plant, its dry weight, is composed principally of oxygen, carbon, and hydrogen.

There are twelve other elements needed for plant growth. Six of these elements—nitrogen, sulfur, phosphorus, calcium, potassium, and magnesium—are needed in relatively large quantities. The other six (called the microelements)—iron, manganese, zinc, copper, boron, and molybdenum—are needed only in extremely small amounts.

The dried leaves, stem, and fruits of a typical plant, corn, have been found to be composed of a number of elements in the following proportions:

ELEMENTS FOUND IN A CORN PLANT

Element	% of Dry Weight	Element	% of Dry Weight
Oxygen	44.43%	Magnesium	0.18
Carbon	43.57	Sulfur	0.17
Hydrogen	6.24	Chlorine	0.14
Nitrogen	1.46	Aluminum	0.11
Silicon	1.17	Iron	0.08
Potassium	0.92	Manganese	0.04
Calcium	0.23	Undetermined (including zinc, copper, boron, molybdenum)	0.93
Phosphorus	0.20		

Any element present in the soil is likely to be absorbed by plant roots. At least 60 elements have thus far been found in plant tissues, and it is likely that every stable element occurs in plants grown under suitable conditions. This fact has led to the development of biogeochemical prospecting. This type of prospecting is done by analyzing the composition of the plants in an area where valuable minerals may exist. The presence in the plant tissue of unusually large amounts of a mineral, such as gold, silver, zinc, or chromium, is a good clue that there may be a deposit of that mineral nearby.

Photo: courtesy Hawaii Press Bureau

PHOTOSYNTHESIS

WE COULD NOT LIVE if there were no green plants, for they are the source of all food. Green plants, such as this sugar cane, can manufacture food from inorganic raw materials. Animals do not possess this ability, and therefore must either feed upon plants or upon other animals which have eaten plants. You may eat plant material in the form of bread, cereal, fruits, and vegetables. Or, when you eat meat, you may eat plant food which has been transformed into the tissues of cattle, sheep, or hogs.

Chlorophyll is the green coloring matter in plants. Its molecules are complex organic networks of over 100 atoms. In some way, these molecules can absorb the energy of sunlight and use it to drive the entire food-making process. This process is called *photosynthesis.* In the first reaction in this process, water is decomposed into hydrogen and oxygen. The oxygen is immediately released into the atmosphere.

Two highly-energized hydrogen atoms which are set free when a molecule of water is decomposed combine with an oxygen atom from carbon dioxide and form a new water molecule. Two other hydrogen atoms combine with the remaining portion of the carbon dioxide molecule to form a basic sugar unit (CH_2O). These basic sugar units are subsequently used to build more complex molecules of the various food substances: carbohydrates, fats, and proteins. Each unit contains a small store of sun energy which has been converted to chemical energy. Later, when the foods which are composed of these units are oxidized in our bodies, the sun energy is released for our use.

Photo: Jessie Lunger from Black Star

VITAMINS

STOP-AND-GO LIGHTS regulate the flow of traffic on our highways. Thermostats regulate the temperature of our homes and offices. In a similar way, vitamins seem to regulate many of the processes within our bodies.

Vitamins, or the compounds which unite to form them, are primarily carbon compounds. They are produced only by plants. The final step in their synthesis, however, may occur within our bodies. Because many vitamins are stored by animals, we obtain them from meats, dairy products, and other animal foods.

Vitamins are needed only in very small quantities. They furnish the body with neither energy nor building materials. But without vitamins the body is unable to utilize properly the foods it receives. Various "deficiency" diseases, such as scurvy, beriberi or pellagra may result from a lack of certain vitamins. A well-balanced diet is the best protection against these diseases.

Before their chemical composition was discovered, vitamins were identified by letters. Even today most vitamins are known by the letter names. Among the vitamins in your diet are:

Vitamin A ($C_{20}H_{30}O$). Promotes growth, good vision, healthy condition of nose, mouth, and internal organ linings. Obtained by eating liver, dairy products, and certain vegetables.

Vitamin B₁ or Thiamine ($C_{12}H_{18}ON_4SC_{12}$). Promotes appetite, vital to growth and reproduction; regulates utilization of carbohydrates by body; prevents beriberi, a crippling disease. Supplied by milk, green vegetables, egg yolks, meats, and yeast.

Vitamin D ($C_{27}H_{43}OH$). Regulates the body's use of calcium and phosphorus; promotes the growth of strong teeth and bones; prevents rickets. Supplied by dairy products and fish. Also synthesized in the body from simpler compounds in the skin under the influence of sunlight.

Photos: Ewing Galloway; National Dairy Council

CHAPTER III

ENERGY EVERYWHERE

SCIENTISTS have not yet discovered exactly what energy is. They define it only in terms of what it does. Generally, they say, energy is a certain "something" which can do work, can be converted into heat, or can produce a change in matter.

Your family buys energy in several forms. Each month, bills for energy arrive from your grocer, electric power company, gas company, coal dealer, and gasoline company. In the following pages you will learn more about the forms of energy with which you are familiar. And, perhaps, you will learn about some forms of energy which you did not know before.

Photo: Ontario Hydro

ENERGY OF MOTION

THE ACTION of this game was stopped as the second baseman threw the ball to home plate for a double play. The speeding ball, caught in mid-air by the camera, possesses energy of motion. This active form of energy, known as kinetic energy, is a characteristic of rolling wheels, expanding gases, running water, flying birds, whirling electrons, galloping horses, and all moving objects.

Kinetic energy is a function of the mass of the moving object and the square of its velocity (see page 124). The mathematical equation to determine the kinetic energy is: $K.E. = \dfrac{mass \times (velocity)^2}{2}$. This equation is merely a simplified statement of easily observed facts. You know that two objects traveling at the same speed may have very different energy levels, depending upon their masses. For example, you would hasten to get out of the path of a bus traveling 20 miles per hour, but a leaf carried along by the wind at the same speed might not even cause you to duck.

Kinetic energy quadruples each time velocity doubles. Therefore, you must allow about four times as much distance to stop your automobile each time you double its speed. Your brakes can stop your car in a distance of 84 feet at 30 miles per hour but they require a distance of 300 feet at 60 miles per hour. The distance your car travels between the time you see danger and the time you apply the brake also lengthens as the car's speed increases.

Photo: H. Armstrong Roberts

STORED ENERGY

POTENTIAL ENERGY is energy stored in an object by reason of its position, condition, or chemical composition. A boy in a tree possesses energy because of his position. The tightly wound spring in your wrist watch and the compressed gas in an air rifle possess energy because of their condition. And a stick of dynamite or a tankful of gasoline possesses energy because of its chemical composition.

Potential energy is measured in terms of the amount of work that could be done by an object. But such a measure is only relative. For example, a rock resting on a table is capable of falling downward under the influence of gravity. It, therefore, has potential energy equal to its weight times the vertical distance through which it can fall. We could calculate the value of the rock's potential energy by multiplying its weight by its distance above the floor. However, we would obtain a considerably different value if its potential energy were calculated on the basis of height of the rock above the ground, especially if the table is in an upper story room of a tall building.

If a suspended object—such as the boy in the apple tree—begins to fall, it loses potential energy as it descends. As its velocity increases, however, the object gains kinetic energy. When the object reaches the bottom of its fall, all of its potential energy has been converted into kinetic energy.

Photo: Ewing Galloway

HEAT ENERGY

THE MOLECULES of every substance are in constant motion, vibrating in place, or slipping and sliding over one another. The kinetic energy of these molecules is known as heat. As the velocity of its molecules increases, the temperature of a body increases. As their velocity decreases, the temperature of the body decreases.

The earth's most important source of heat is the sun. But many earthly reactions also release heat. For instance, the oxidation of coal releases sufficient energy to increase the velocity of the air molecules in your home and to keep you warm through the winter.

Heat is transferred from place to place by conduction, convection, and radiation. *Conduction* is the transfer of energy from more-rapidly moving (hotter) molecules to more sluggish (colder) ones by direct contact. It occurs between the molecules of matter in all states, but some matter conducts heat much better than other matter. Good conductors are used in cooking utensils, heating equipment, engines, and other items. Poor conductors are used to prevent the transfer of heat. Asbestos, for example, is made into protective clothing for industrial workers and fire fighters. It is also used to insulate homes against heat loss.

Convection consists of the movement of heated portions of a substance due to expansion and the consequent reduction of density that accompany heating. Therefore, convection can occur only in liquids and gases. Air warmed by the furnace rises and flows out through the registers to warm your home by convection.

Radiation, unlike the other methods, does not require the presence of matter to effect an energy transfer. For example, energy from the sun is radiated in the form of electromagnetic waves to the earth through space (see page 92). Long waves, called infra-red waves, produce the sensation of warmth. These waves are continually emitted from a body and may be absorbed, reflected from, or transmitted through other bodies which they strike. If they are absorbed by a body, the body is heated.

Photo: courtesy Johns-Mansville

LIGHT ENERGY

Sunlight falling upon this "solar battery" is transformed to electricity to operate a rural telephone system. Surplus electricity, stored as chemical energy in batteries, is used to power the system after dark. Because it can be transformed into electrical, chemical, and other forms of energy, light must itself be a form of energy.

The primary sources of light are very hot objects, such as the sun and stars; light-bulb filaments and other incandescent solids; and burning fuels. But light is also produced by slow oxidation—for example, the eerie light of the firefly—and by the passage of electricity through a rare gas, as in the neon tubes used in advertising signs.

The exact nature of light is one of the greatest unknowns of modern science. However, scientists believe that light is produced by activity within the atoms of the light source. When an atom receives additional energy, by collisions with other atoms or in some other way, its electrons are deflected from their normal paths to paths more distant from the nucleus. The electrons subsequently lose energy by radiation and return to their normal paths. The infinitesimal quantity of radiation emitted from a single electron is known as a *quantum*. Quanta seem to travel in waves which are similar in form to the ripples produced when a pebble is dropped into the quiet waters of a lake. These waves are known as electromagnetic waves. The distance between two successive crests is known as the length of the wave.

Electromagnetic waves with very short wave lengths (0.000000001 cm. to 0.0000005 cm.) are known as X-rays, others with much longer wave lengths (0.00007 cm. to 0.03 cm.) are called infra-red or heat waves. Light waves are electromagnetic waves of intermediate lengths (0.000035 cm. to 0.00007 cm.) which produce vision. Electromagnetic waves travel 186,320.69 miles per second or 670,754,520 miles per hour. At this speed, light could travel from New York City to San Francisco and back again 36 times in one second.

Photo: courtesy Bell Telephone

BENDING LIGHT

LIGHT RAYS which strike a piece of glass obliquely are bent as they pass through the glass. This bending, which also occurs when light passes through water, plastic, or other transparent substances, is known as refraction.

Our knowledge of refraction has led to the development of lenses. A lens is essentially a transparent object with two opposite, smooth surfaces. These surfaces may both be curved, or one may be curved and the other flat.

There are two classes of lenses: *Converging lenses* have convex surfaces. They are thicker at the center than at their edges. When parallel rays of light pass through a lens of this type they are bent inward. Therefore, the rays converge at a point beyond the lens, the principal focus. The distance between the lens and this focus point is known as the focal length of the lens. It decreases as the lens becomes more convex. An inverted image of the object from which the light was reflected or emitted is produced behind the principal focus point. Such an image, which can be seen on a sheet of paper held in the proper position, is termed a real image.

Diverging lenses are concave. Their edges are thicker than their centers. When parallel rays of light pass through a lens of this kind, they are bent outward. Because the rays diverge, no real image is formed by this type of lens. However, if the axes of the diverging rays are extended back through the lens, they meet at an imaginary principal focus point which is located on the same side of the lens as the light source. The upright image that appears to be produced between the object and the lens is known as a virtual image. It cannot be projected onto a sheet of paper.

Lenses are found in the eyes of nearly every animal, in eyeglasses, telescopes, microscopes, binoculars, magnifying glasses, cameras, motion picture projectors, and many other optical instruments.

Photo: courtesy Corning Glass Works

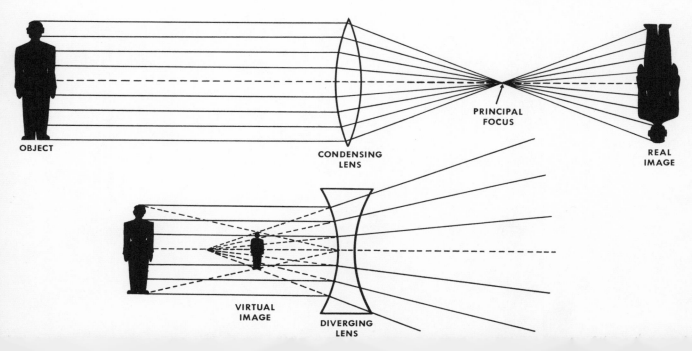

OBJECT

CONDENSING
LENS

PRINCIPAL
FOCUS

REAL
IMAGE

VIRTUAL
IMAGE

DIVERGING
LENS

EYES

Eyes are marvelous devices. They allow us to investigate the mystery of a tiny snowflake or to explore visually hundreds of millions of miles into space as we gaze at the starlit skies. Nevertheless, the mechanical design of an eye is simple. Basically, five parts allow us to see:

The cornea is the transparent, protective cover which admits light to the eye. Because it is convex, it acts as a lens to focus light.

The iris is a muscular disk situated between the cornea and the lens. An opening at the center of the iris (the pupil) automatically regulates the intensity of light reaching the lens. In bright light the pupil closes, allowing only a pinpoint of light to pass. In dim light the pupil opens wide, to allow a large portion of the light to enter.

The crystalline lens, a converging lens, focuses light on the retina, producing an inverted image of the scene being viewed. By muscular action, the lens can be made more convex or more flat. This allows your eye to focus on objects only a few inches away or on objects many miles away.

The retina is the light-sensitive tissue which lines the interior of your eye. The cells of the retina translate the visual light image into a series of electrochemical nerve impulses.

The optic nerve has many branches in the retina which receive nerve impulses and transmit them to the brain. The brain unscrambles these impulses, reinverts the image and interprets the scene for us.

Photo: Rudy Terry

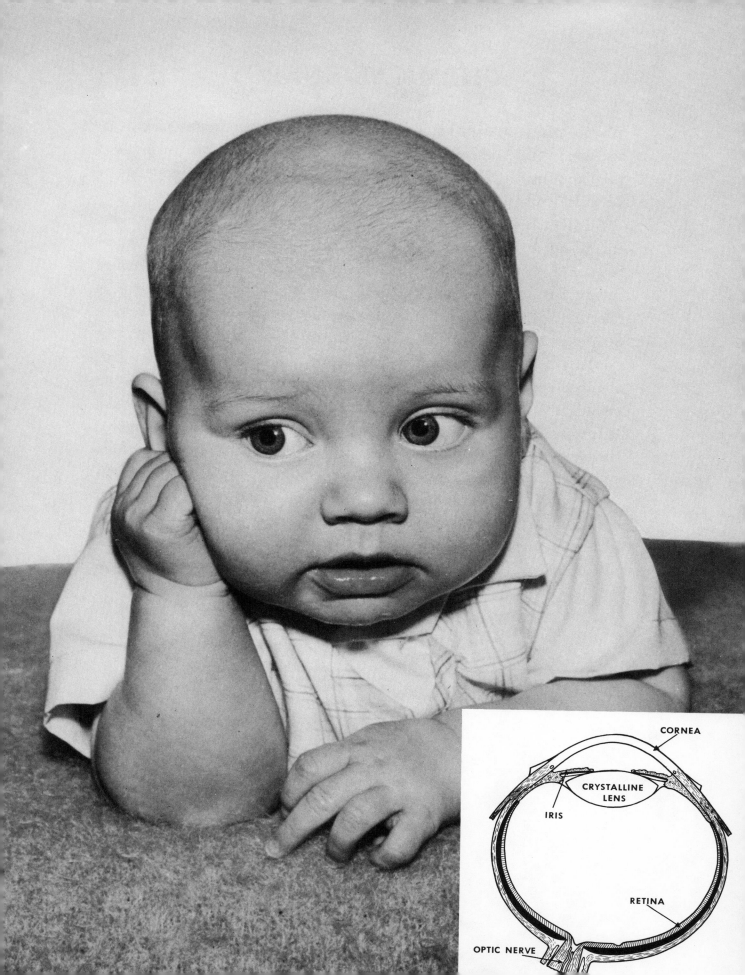

CORNEA

CRYSTALLINE LENS

IRIS

RETINA

OPTIC NERVE

CHEMICAL ENERGY

WE DO NOT PURCHASE gasoline merely to manufacture water vapor, carbon dioxide, and other exhaust gases. Nor do we burn coal just to produce gases and smoke which rise up through the chimney. We are interested in the energy that these fuels contain.

All substances possess chemical energy, energy in a potential form. This energy can be transformed to a usable, kinetic form through a chemical reaction. Coal, gasoline, and fuel oil are burned to release their chemical energy. The chemical energy of food, which is used by all living things, is released by slow oxidation. The matches in this photograph will release their store of energy almost instantly when they are struck.

Many chemical reactions are endothermic, that is, they absorb heat. This absorbed energy is apparently used to bind the atoms of the resulting compounds into molecules. It is released when the molecules are decomposed. It is often desirable to convert energy in other forms to more easily-stored chemical energy. For example, during the process of photosynthesis, light energy from the sun is transformed to chemical energy in simple sugars. These sugars may be used to build plant tissue. Animals which eat plants oxidize these tissues during the process of digestion, releasing some of the solar energy which was stored in them.

Photo: courtesy Diamond Match Co.

ELECTRICAL ENERGY

PIECES OF PAPER will jump toward a comb that has been passed through your hair. A glass rod stroked with silk also attracts light objects. In this condition, the comb and glass are said to be electrically charged.

Charged glass will attract a charged comb, but will repel other charged glass. Charged combs also repel one another. Thus, there are two kinds of electrical charges. *Unlike charges attract; like charges repel.* A charge which behaves like that on glass is called a positive charge. One which behaves like that on a comb is called a negative charge.

Static electricity is electricity residing in an object. When objects with opposite charges are connected, electricity flows between them. This moving electricity is an electric current. The energy of moving electricity is used to light cities, to power industry, and to run thousands of machines which ease our daily chores. The plight of a modern family deprived of electricity is humorously shown in this cartoon.

There are two kinds of electric currents. A direct current (D.C.) flows only in one direction. An alternating current (A.C.) flows first in one direction and then in the other. One complete back-and-forth movement is known as a cycle. Ordinary house current is 60-cycle A.C., that is, the direction of flow is reversed 120 times each second.

Substances through which an electric current can flow are called conductors. The atoms of a conductor have electrons or ions which can move about. When they move in the same direction, due to a "push" supplied by a battery or generator, an electric current flows through the conductor. Non-conducting substances, called insulators, are comprised of atoms whose electrons are immobile, or compounds which do not ionize.

When you use a comb, electrons pass to it from your hair. The comb, oversupplied with electrons, becomes negatively charged. Your hair is left with a positive charge. A similar exchange takes place between glass and silk, except that electrons are transferred to the cloth and the glass is left with a positive charge.

MAGNETS

A MAGNET is an object which exerts a measurable attraction for iron, steel, and a few other substances. Lodestone, an iron ore, is a natural magnet. Artificial magnets are made from iron, steel, and mixtures of nickel, iron, and other metals.

If iron filings are sprinkled on a magnet, most of them adhere to its ends or poles. When a straight magnet, such as a compass needle, is free to rotate it will come to rest with one end pointing north. Near this end is its *north pole*. Near the other end is its *south pole*. Unlike poles (north and south) of magnets attract and like poles repel one another.

The space through which a magnet is effective is its magnetic field. If iron filings are sprinkled on a paper which has been laid over a bar magnet, the filings align themselves in paths which indicate lines of force of the magnetic field (Figure 1). These lines run through space from the north to the south pole and continue through the magnet.

The exact nature of magnetism is unknown. We know that if a magnet is broken, each piece acts as a magnet. Even small groups of molecules (domains) of a magnetic substance must act as magnets, each with a north and a south pole. The domains of an unmagnetized object are haphazardly arranged (Figure 2). If the object is stroked with a magnet, the domains turn so that all of their north poles point in the same direction (Figure 3). The object then behaves as a magnet.

A body charged with static electricity possesses no special magnetic properties, but moving electricity creates a magnetic field about it. The lines of force form concentric circles around a straight wire (Figure 4). If the wire is wound into a coil, the lines merge into a powerful magnetic field similar to that of a bar magnet. Such a coil is known as a solenoid. The solenoid is the basic element of the electromagnet. Some electromagnets are very large, such as this one which is lifting several hundred pounds of scrap iron. Others, such as those in door bells and telephone receivers, are very small.

Photo: Ewing Galloway

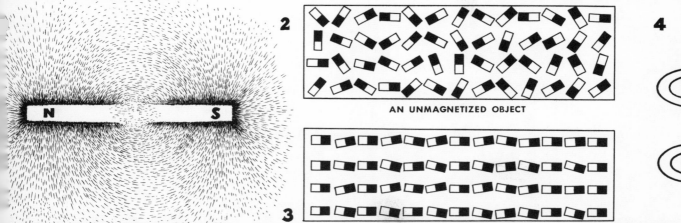

A MAGNETIC FIELD ABOUT A BAR MAGNET

2 AN UNMAGNETIZED OBJECT

3 A MAGNETIZED OBJECT

4 MAGNETIC FIELD AROUND A WIRE

GRAVITATION

GRAVITATION is a pull exerted by any two objects upon one another. Every particle of matter in the universe attracts every other particle with a force which is directly proportional to the product of their masses, and inversely proportional to the square of the distance between their centers.

The gravitational force between all but the largest bodies is quite small. For example, the force between two battleships side by side would be less than one pound. But the force between the planets and stars in the universe is fantastically great. In fact, the force of gravitation holds the universe together.

The attraction between the earth and bodies on or near its surface is known as *gravity*. This force is responsible for the weight of various objects. It also prevents them from hurtling out into space. Of the countless practical uses of gravity, one of the most interesting is the elevator. Perhaps you have noticed that as an elevator goes up, a small box-like object glides down a special rail at the rear of the elevator shaft. When the elevator comes down, the box rises. This box is sufficiently heavy to balance the weight of the loaded elevator car. Therefore, the mechanism which raises the car is supplemented by the potential energy of the balance weight.

However, the most fundamental question is still unanswerable: What causes gravitation?

Photo: courtesy Otis Elevator Co.

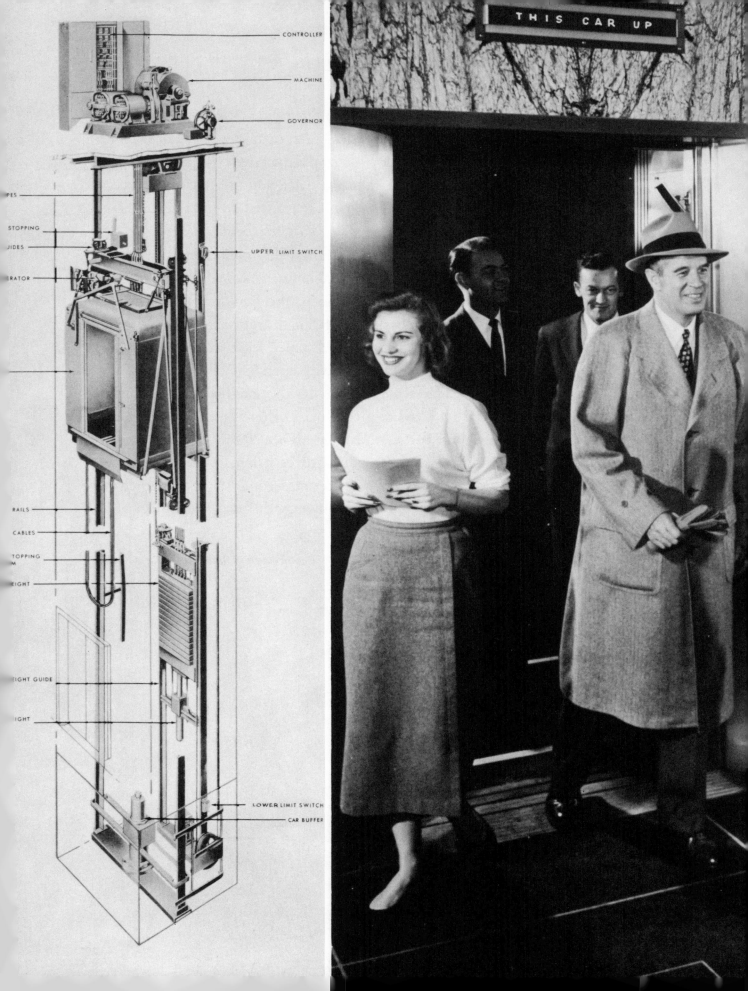

CONTROLLER

MACHINE

GOVERNOR

PES

STOPPING

JIDES

ERATOR

UPPER LIMIT SWITCH

RAILS

CABLES

TOPPING
M

EIGHT

EIGHT GUIDE

IGHT

LOWER LIMIT SWITCH

CAR BUFFER

THIS CAR UP

FORCE

A FORCE is a push or a pull that acts upon an object. A force may tend to cause a resting object to move. It may accelerate a moving object or change its direction of motion. It may slow or stop a moving object. Or it may produce distortion in an object. Gravity and friction are common forces. All bodily movements are the result of forces exerted by muscles. These horses are exerting a force upon the wagon they are pulling.

Force is measured in the English system by the gravitational unit, the pound (see page 120). A pound is the force of attraction which the earth's gravity exerts upon a standard mass of one pound. In the metric system (see page 114), the gram is the basic gravitational unit of force.

Gravitational units of force vary with distance from the center of the earth. Therefore, a series of absolute units, independent of gravity, is also used to measure force. The absolute unit of the English system is the poundal. It is the force required to give a mass of one pound an acceleration of one foot per second per second. The absolute unit of force in the metric system is the dyne, the force which gives a mass of one gram an acceleration of one centimeter per second per second. A pound force is about 32 times as large as a poundal, while a gram force is equal to 980 dynes.

Photo: courtesy Standard Oil Co. (N.J.)

THE CONVERSION AND CONSERVATION OF ENERGY

An important series of energy transformations takes place in a hydro-electric plant, such as this one at Hungry Horse Dam, Montana. Water stored in the reservoir behind the tall dam has tremendous potential energy. When it drops nearly 600 feet through a long tubular flume to the base of the dam, the water's potential energy is changed to kinetic energy.

At the bottom of this flume the rushing water pushes against the paddles or blades of a huge turbine wheel and causes the wheel to rotate. The energy of running water is thereby converted to rotational energy. As the turbine wheel rotates, it turns the shaft to which it is attached. Then, in a room high above the turbine, the other end of the turning shaft drives a generator which converts mechanical to electrical energy. The electricity produced by four of these turbine-powered generators travels over wires to homes and factories throughout the region surrounding this dam.

This series of energy transformations illustrates a universal principle: *energy can readily be converted from one form to another*. Other examples are: the burning of coal, which converts chemical energy to heat and light energy; the work of an electric motor, which changes electric energy to mechanical energy; and the conversion of light energy to chemical energy by the activity of green plants.

A second principle, which is inseparably associated with conversion of energy, is that of conservation of energy. Basically, this principle states: *while energy can be changed from one form to another, the total amount of energy in a closed system remains unchanged*. For example, the work done by a machine, plus the frictional loss within the machine, always equals the effort put into the machine.

Photo: A. E. McCloud from Bureau of Reclamation

WATER

FLUME

GENERATOR
OF ELECTRIC
CURRENT

DAM

TURBINE
WHEEL

SOUND

THROUGHOUT LIFE we are surrounded by sounds—sounds of human voices, sounds of the city, sounds of the farm. We learn to identify sounds and to communicate our desires, opinions, passions, and knowledge by them.

But what are sounds? They are series of compressions in an elastic medium, such as air, water, wood, or steel, produced by a vibrating body. The vibrating body may be the vocal chords of a human throat, the tight skin of a drum, a column of air in an organ pipe, or any one of many other objects.

In the horn at the left of this picture, the vibrating body is a small metal diaphragm. As the diaphragm flexes outward, it pushes the molecules of the air closer together, forming an area of compression. As it flexes inward, it momentarily reduces pressure and the air molecules move farther apart. The energy transmitted from the vibrating diaphragm to adjacent air molecules is transferred from molecule to molecule by billions of collisions. In this way, compression waves separated by bands of low pressure are beamed out from the loudspeaker. A special device was used to change these sound waves to ribbons of light. The bright lines are compressions. In the darker areas between these lines the air molecules have spread apart farther than normal.

You have undoubtedly noticed that a flash of lightning is always seen before thunder is heard, and smoke is seen discharged from a distant gun before the shot is heard. These observations indicate that sound travels at a speed slower than that of light (186,321 miles per second). Careful measurements have shown that the speed of sound is only 1,090 feet per second or 741.3 miles per hour in air at 0° C. (32° F.). Its speed increases by about 2 feet per second (1.4 miles per hour) for each degree centrigrade rise in air temperature and decreases by 2 feet per second with every degree drop in air temperature.

Photo: courtesy Bell Telephone

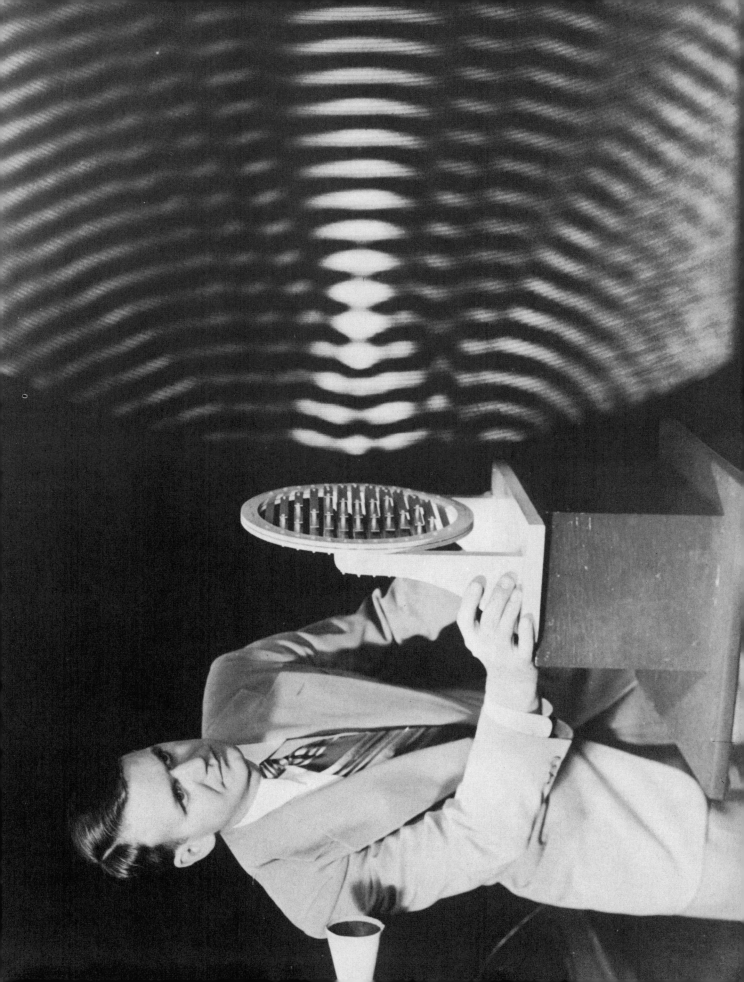

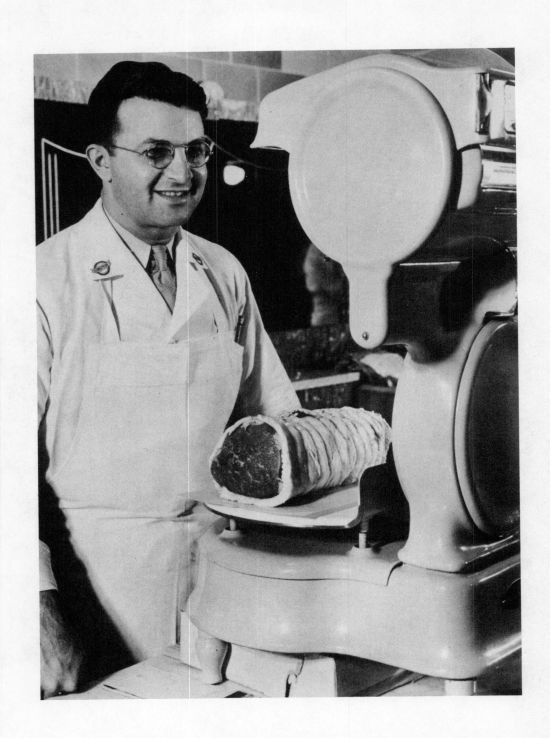

CHAPTER IV

HOW WE MEASURE

IN OUR DAILY ACTIVITIES we repeatedly make use of measurements. At the grocery, a housewife buys a *quart* of milk, a *pound* of meat, a 5-*fluid ounce* bottle of sauce and, if she is a bit overweight, perhaps a carton of soft drinks advertised as low in *calories*. A man figures the distance from home to the office in *miles,* and the speed of his car in *miles per hour.* He buys gasoline by the *gallon,* wire by the *foot,* rugs by the *square yard,* land by the *acre,* cooking gas by the *cubic foot,* and coal by the *ton.*

It is clear that the complex system of exchange in our modern civilization would be impossible without adequate measurements. The houses we live in and the buildings in which we learn, work, worship, and play would never have been built if men had not been able to measure each part to fit properly to the next.

Science as we know it did not—could not—exist until men developed methods by which to measure distance, area, volume, temperature, heat, time, and other quantities.

Photo: Ewing Galloway

DISTANCE

Whether he calculates the distance to the next village or to a star, man needs a way to measure and express length and distance. Because these are measurements of lines, they are called *linear* measurements.

Parts of the body are convenient units for linear measurement. For centuries a system of measures was used which included: the digit, the width of the index finger; the foot, the length of the human foot; and the cubit, the distance from the tip of the middle finger to the elbow. But people differ in stature. So the measurements varied from person to person. In the 15th century, the British government standardized the units of length, volume, and weight so that they would mean the same thing to all people. This system, known as the *English system,* is still used in the United States and other English-speaking countries.

English units originated haphazardly and are not related systematically. For example, 12 inches equal one foot, and a mile contains 63,360 inches or 5,280 feet. As you can see, it is difficult to convert measurements from one unit to another.

About 1800, the French developed a new system of measurement, the *metric system.* The basic linear unit, the meter, was defined as one ten-millionth of the distance from the North Pole to the equator. Other units, including those of volume and weight, are based upon the meter. All units are decimally related. That is, they increase or decrease by multiples of ten. Their names are formed with Greek prefixes. Thus a *centimeter* is .01 meter, a *decimeter* is .1 meter, a *dekameter* is 10 meters, a *hectameter* is 100 meters and a *kilometer* is 1,000 meters.

The metric system is used in many countries. It is the system accepted by scientists throughout the world.

ENGLISH LINEAR UNITS
1 inch (in.) = 2.54 centimeters
12 in. = 1 foot (ft.) = 30.48 centimeters
3 ft. = 1 yard (yd.) = 9.14 decimeters
5,280 ft. = 1 mile (mi.) = 1.609 kilometers

METRIC LINEAR UNITS
1 millimeter (mm.) = 0.03937 inches
10 mm. = 1 centimeter (cm.) = 0.3937 inches
10 cm. = 1 meter (m.) = 3.28 feet
1,000 m. = 1 kilometer (km.) = 3,280.83 feet

Photo: Standard Oil Co. (N.J.)

US
5

←

SPRINGFIELD 23 M.

WAREHOUSE POINT 9 M.

CO

15

WORCES

ROCKV

WA

AREA

AREA IS A MEASURE of the amount of space on the surface of a figure. While linear measurements consider only one dimension (length), areal measurements consider two: length and width. Width is a linear measurement made at a right angle to the measurement of length.

Area is derived from the measurements of length and width (length x width = area). For example, this page is 10.8 inches long (27.5 cm.) and 8.2 inches wide (20.8 cm.). Its area, therefore, is 88.6 square inches (10.8 x 8.2), or 572 square centimeters.

Length and width must be expressed in the same unit before they can be multiplied to obtain area. Length in inches will yield a measurement of area only when multiplied by the width in inches. Because a linear unit, such as an inch, has to be multiplied by itself (squared) to obtain a unit of area, area is not expressed in inches or similar linear units, but in *squares* of those units—for example, square inches.

Measurements of area are of extreme importance in all fields of science. They are also used in real estate transactions because the price of a parcel of land is largely determined by its size (area). A farmer must know the area of his fields to calculate the amount of seed and fertilizer needed to grow his crops. Foresters, engineers, architects, builders, and people in many other occupations deal with measurements of area. Some of the areal units of the English and metric systems are compared in the following tables.

SQUARE MEASURES—*English System*

	1 square inch (sq. in)	= 6.4516 sq. cm.
144 sq. in.	= 1 square foot (sq. ft.)	= 929.00 sq. cm.
9 sq. ft.	= 1 square yard (sq. yd.)	= 0.8361 sq. m.
4,840 sq. yd.	= 1 acre (A.)	= 4,046.87 sq. m.
640 A.	= 1 square mile (sq. mi.)	= 2.5899 sq. km.

SQUARE MEASURES—*Metric System*

	1 square millimeter (sq. mm. or mm²)	= 0.00155 sq. in.
100 mm²	= 1 square centimeter (sq. cm. or cm²)	= 0.155 sq. in.
100 cm²	= 1 square decimeter (sq. dm. or dm²)	= 15.50 sq. in.
100 dm²	= 1 square meter (sq. m. or m²)	= 10.764 sq. ft.
1,000,000 m²	= 1 square kilometer (sq. km. or km²)	= 0.3861 sq. mi.

Photo: Jack McCormick

FOR SALE
47 ACRES
1900 FT. FRONTAGE
SKILLMAN & SKILLMAN
247 NASSAU ST. PRINCETON, N.J.
PHONE-PR. 1-3822

VOLUME AND CAPACITY

VOLUME, the space occupied by a substance, is an important quantity in science and commerce. While solids are usually measured by weight (you buy sugar and flour by the pound, and coal and steel by the ton), liquids and gases are more easily measured by volume. At the filling station, therefore, you do not buy gasoline by the pound but by the gallon. Milk is sold by the quart. Cooking gas is purchased by the cubic foot.

Volume is a three-dimensional concept derived from length, width, and thickness (length x width x thickness = volume). Length and width are measurements of a plane, such as the floor of a room. Thickness is a measurement made perpendicular to that plane. The "thickness" of the room, then, is the distance from floor to ceiling. By multiplying together the length, width, and thickness of a room you can determine the volume of air it contains.

In determining volume, all measurements must be computed in the same linear unit, such as an inch or meter. Because this unit is multiplied by itself twice (cubed), units of volume are not expressed as inches or meters, but as *cubic* inches, cubic meters, and so on.

Units of volume or special units are used to measure the capacity of a container, such as a tank or box. Two special series of English units are employed to measure the capacity of a container, one for dry substances and one for fluids. A few of these units are shown with other volumetric units of the English and metric systems in the following table.

CUBIC MEASURE—*English System*

	1 cubic inch (cu. in.)	= 16.3872 cu. cm.
1728 cu. in. =	1 cubic foot (cu. ft.)	= 0.0283 cu. m.
27 cu. ft. =	1 cubic yard (cu. yd.)	= 0.7645 cu. m.

LIQUID CAPACITY—*English System*

	1 fluid ounce (fl. oz.)	= 0.02957 liter
16 fl. oz. =	1 liquid pint (pt.)	= 0.4732 liter
2 pt. =	1 liquid quart (qt.)	= 0.9463 liter
4 qt. =	1 gallon (gal.)	= 3.7853 liters

DRY CAPACITY—*English System*

	1 dry pint (dry pt.)	= 0.5506 liter
2 dry pt. =	1 dry quart (dry qt.)	= 1.1012 liters
32 dry qt. =	1 bushel (bu.)	= 35.2383 liters

CUBIC MEASURE AND CAPACITY—*Metric System*

1 cubic centimeter (cc) = 1 millimeter (ml) = 0.061 cu. in.
1 cubic decimeter (cu. dm.) = 1,000 ml = 1 liter (l) = 61.025 cu. in.
1 cubic meter = 1,000 l = 1 kiloliter (kl) 35.314 cu. ft. = 264.178 gal.

MASS AND WEIGHT

THE DOWNWARD PULL exerted by gravity on any particular object is known as the weight of that object. Weight is directly related to the quantity of matter contained in an object, or its mass. Hence, an object with a mass of two units weighs twice as much as an object with a mass of one unit. Weight, therefore, is a convenient measure of mass.

The most common devices for measuring weight are the beam balance and spring scale. A beam balance is a first-class lever (see page 138) with arms of equal length. A weight at the end of one arm will exactly balance an equal weight at the end of the other arm. Standard units of mass, in the form of brass cylinders, are used to balance objects whose weight is to be determined.

Spring scales employ a steel spring or some other elastic material to measure weight. Such a scale must be calibrated with known masses. Then, unknown objects which affect the spring to the same degree as a known mass are considered to be equal to that mass.

Weight decreases as the distance of the object from the earth's center increases. Mass remains constant. Therefore, while mass can be determined accurately in any location by comparison with standard units of mass on a balance, a spring scale is accurate only at the place at which it was originally calibrated.

The metric system derived its basic weight unit, the *gram,* from the mass of one cubic centimeter of pure water. The units of weight in the English system were based upon the mass of a cubic foot of water. One thousandth of this mass was called an *ounce.* The weight of 16 cubic feet of water was designated as 1,000 *pounds.* The original measurements were slightly in error, however, and 1,000 modern ounces actually weigh slightly less than a cubic foot of water.

WEIGHT—*English System*

	1 ounce (oz.)	= 28.35 g
16 oz.	= 1 pound (lb.)	= 453.59
2,000 lbs.	= 1 short ton (sh. t.)	= 0.9 metric t

WEIGHT—*Metric System*

	1 gram (g)	= 0.04 oz.
1,000 g	= 1 kilogram (kg)	= 2.20 lbs.
1,000,000 g	= 1 metric ton (t)	= 2,204.62 lbs.

Photo: courtesy Toledo Scale Co.

TIME

BOTH THE ENGLISH and metric systems employ the same units to measure time. These units are based on the mean solar day, the average period between two successive solar noons. Solar noon at a given place is the precise instant when the sun appears to pass through an imaginary plane which extends from that place to the earth's north and south geographical poles.

The mean solar day is divided into 24 equal parts, called *hours*. Each hour is divided into 60 *minutes* and each minute, in turn, is divided into 60 *seconds*.

Seven solar days constitute one *week*. And a *year* is approximately 365¼ days in length. This fractional day is accommodated by adding an extra day to each fourth year. This 366-day-long year is known as "leap year."

All measurements of time are based on exacting observations of solar movements. However, the most popular time-keeping devices are clocks. They are made in an amazing array of sizes and shapes. But all clocks are based on the same principle: If the circumstances are exactly the same, a given object requires precisely the same time to move through a specified distance in one case as in another. Thus, the hands of a clock, in one hour, move through exactly the same distance as they did in the hour before and as they will in each hour afterward. Of course, this principle is exemplified by the apparent movement of the sun upon which our measurements of time are based.

Photo: courtesy Elgin Watch Company

SPEED, VELOCITY, AND ACCELERATION

Speed and velocity are often used interchangeably to describe the rate at which something moves. Scientists, however, use these terms to express two different but closely related concepts.

Speed is the rate of motion of a body, stated as the distance traveled in a given time. Average speed is calculated by dividing the distance traveled by the time required to travel that distance. A huge Viking rocket travels for a brief time at nearly 4,400 miles per hour (m.p.h.). A runner may be clocked at 20.2 seconds in the Olympic 200-meter dash, an average speed of 9.9 meters per second.

Scientists employ Mach numbers (pronounced mock) to measure high speeds. A Mach number is the ratio of an object's speed to the speed of sound, Mach 1. Mach .8 is less than the speed of sound (subsonic). Mach 3 is three times as fast as the speed of sound (supersonic). Because the speed of sound varies with the temperature, Mach 1 may be equal to 700 m.p.h. at sea level on a cold day and over 800 m.p.h. on a hot day. In the cold air at high altitudes, Mach 1 may be equivalent to a speed of only 660 m.p.h.

As a plane pushes through the air, it sets up a series of shock waves which travel at the speed of sound. If a plane breaks the sound barrier, that is, if it exceeds Mach 1, the waves pile up in front of the plane, making it difficult to handle. When the waves reach the ear of a person on the ground, he hears a deafening explosion.

The velocity of a body is its speed in a given direction. The velocity of an express train on a straight stretch of track, for example, might be 96 m.p.h. toward the northwest. A change in velocity occurs when there is a change in speed or direction. The rate of change of speed is termed acceleration, and it may be positive (increased speed) or negative (decreased speed). For example, if the speed of an automobile is increased from 35 m.p.h. to 55 m.p.h. in two minutes, the speed is increased 20 miles per hour. The acceleration during this change of speed is 10 miles per hour per minute.

Photo: Ewing Galloway

WORK AND POWER

IN SCIENCE, work is defined as a transfer of energy which involves movement of the point to which a force is applied.

Work is measured by the product of the force exerted upon an object and the distance through which the force moves (work = force x distance). The quantity of work can be expressed by any unit of force multiplied by any unit of distance. Measurements are commonly given in *gram-centimeters* or in *foot-pounds*. For example, a laborer does 1,500 foot-pounds of work when he carries a 30-pound stone up a 50-foot-high hill (30 lbs. x 50 ft.).

Another unit of work is the *erg,* which is the work done when a force of one dyne (see page 106) is exerted through a distance of one centimeter. An erg is approximately equal to the work done when a mosquito is lifted three-eighths of an inch. The *joule,* which is equal to 10 million ergs, is a more convenient unit for most purposes. It is also equal to 0.738 foot-pounds.

Power is the rate at which work is done. It is determined by dividing the quantity of work by the period of time during which the work was done (average power = work ÷ time). *Horsepower* is a common unit used to measure the power of various engines. It is equal to 550 foot-pounds per second, 76 kilogram-meters per second, or 746 watts. The watt, which equals one joule per second, and the kilowatt (1,000 watts) are commonly used to measure the power of electric motors, generators, and lights.

Photo: courtesy United Nations

TEMPERATURE

NEARLY EVERY SUBSTANCE expands when it is heated and contracts to its original size when it is cooled to the starting temperature. On a cold, winter day the Empire State Building in New York City is 1,250 feet tall. But it stretches upward an extra foot when warmed by the midsummer sun. This stretch is an example of thermal expansion, the phenomenon which underlies the operation of the thermometer, an instrument used to measure heat.

Thermometers measure only the intensity of heat. This relative measure gives no indication of the quantity of heat in any body or the differences in total heat possessed by different bodies. Thus, water in a tea kettle may be at the same temperature as water spouting skyward from Old Faithful Geyser in Yellowstone National Park. But the quantity of heat present in the kettle is a small fraction of that in the thousands of gallons of water issuing from the geyser.

Thermometers contain a liquid especially chosen for its expansion properties. Alcohol is used in less-expensive instruments and in those to be used in cold regions, such as at this polar climatic shelter. Mercury is used in medium and high-temperature ranges. All thermometers are calibrated against the temperatures of a mixture of ice and water and of steam.

There are two temperature scales in common use. On one scale, the *centigrade* scale of the metric system, a value of 0° C. is assigned to ice water and 100° C. to steam, with 100 equal units between. On the *Fahrenheit* scale, an English measure, the temperature of ice water is set equal to 32° F. and that of steam to 212° F., with 180 equal units between. The units can be extended above and below the standard temperatures as far as required. Each centigrade degree is equal to 1.8 Fahrenheit degrees. The scales are compared in the diagram. In this book, temperatures are given on the centigrade scale, the scale used by scientists all over the world. Fahrenheit temperatures are given in parentheses.

Photo: courtesy U.S. Air Force

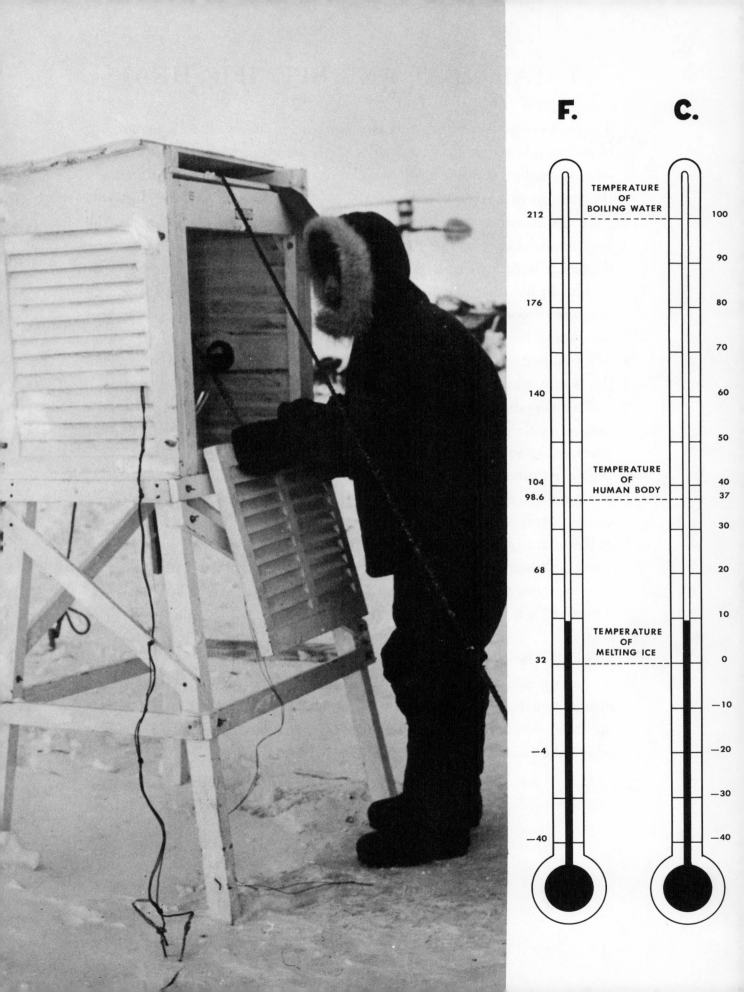

F.

C.

TEMPERATURE
OF
BOILING WATER

212 — — 100

— 90

176 — — 80

— 70

140 — — 60

— 50

TEMPERATURE
OF
HUMAN BODY

104 — — 40
98.6 — — 37

— 30

68 — — 20

— 10

TEMPERATURE
OF
MELTING ICE

32 — — 0

— —10

— —20

−4 — — —30

−40 — — —40

TOTAL HEAT AND SPECIFIC HEAT

TEMPERATURE is a relative measure of heat intensity. It tells us nothing of the total heat present in a body. But temperature measurements are the basis of another series of units which are used to determine quantitatively the amount of heat in a body.

In the metric system the basic unit of heat quantity is the *calorie,* the heat required to raise the temperature of one gram of water one centigrade degree. It is equivalent to 427 gram-meters of mechanical energy.

The British thermal unit (B.t.u.), the heat required to raise the temperature of one pound of water one Fahrenheit degree, is the basic heat measure of the English system. One B.t.u. is equal to 252 calories or to 778 foot-pounds. The British thermal unit is customarily used to measure the heat produced by various fuels, such as coal, oil, gas, and gasoline.

The temperature of one substance may rise much more rapidly than that of another substance when both are subjected to the same heat. For example, to raise the temperature of one gram of water one centigrade degree requires 1.0 calorie. But only one-fifth as much heat is needed to raise the temperature of a similar mass of aluminum one degree (0.22 calorie), and just one-eleventh as much for lead (0.03 calorie). The ratio of the quantity of heat required to raise a given mass of a substance through a given degree of temperature to the quantity required to raise an equal mass of water through the same range is the *specific heat* of the substance. The specific heat of water is 1, that of aluminum is 0.22, and that of lead is 0.03.

Specific heats of various substances are accurately determined in this ice calorimeter at the National Bureau of Standards. The material is first heated to a known temperature in the small cylinder to the left of the operator's head. Then the material is dropped down into the calorimeter where the heat it releases while cooling to 0° C. (32° F.) is measured.

Photo: courtesy National Bureau of Standards

130

ELECTRICITY

PERIODICALLY the "light man" reads the dials of a glass-enclosed electric meter in your home to determine the amount of electrical energy used. Later, his company will send a bill for this energy. The charge is based on the number of kilowatt hours used. In order to understand how much energy a kilowatt hour represents, we must first learn about several units that are more basic.

The number of electrons that pass through a conductor in a given time determines the size of the current. The *ampere* is the unit used to measure electric current. One ampere is equivalent to a flow of about 6.3 billion electrons per second through a conductor.

Every substance resists, more or less, the passage of an electric current. The practical unit of measurement of resistance is the *ohm*. By agreement, it is the resistance offered by a column of mercury 106.3 centimeters (42.2 in.) long, 1 square millimeter (.0016 sq. in.) in cross-sectional area, at 0° C. (32° F.).

Electrons are driven through a conductor by a pressure known as an *electromotive force* (e.m.f.) which is measured in a unit known as the *volt*. One volt equals the e.m.f. that will cause a current of one ampere to flow through a conductor having a resistance of one ohm. Ordinarily, there is an e.m.f. of 110-120 volts in the wires of homes. Lightning involves e.m.f.'s of several million volts.

The *watt* is a unit used to measure the power or rate of consumption of electrical energy. It is the potential rate of work of a current of one ampere maintained by an e.m.f. of one volt (watts = volts x amperes). A 60-watt bulb uses exactly twice as much current as a 30-watt bulb.

Commercially, electrical energy is measured in kilowatt-hours (kw.hr.). One kw.hr. is equivalent to one watt of power delivered for 1,000 hours. This amount of electrical energy will operate a large television set for more than five hours, a 100-watt bulb for ten hours, or an electric toaster for about one hour.

Photos: courtesy Popular Science; General Electric

CHAPTER V

THE PHYSICS OF SIMPLE MACHINES

PRIMITIVE PEOPLES used their hands, feet, heads, and bodies to push and pull objects. When the tasks proved too great, they devised simple tools which multiplied the forces they were able to exert.

Next you will read about the fundamental machines used by man. Over the centuries, these machines have served man in many forms. The most complex machines of modern industry are but combinations of these simple machines.

Drawing by Lewis Brown

THE PRINCIPLE OF THE LEVER

You use a great many levers each day. Scissors, pliers, bottle openers, even parts of your own body are levers. But, what is a lever? It is a rigid object, usually a bar, rod, or pole that is capable of turning about a point called its *fulcrum.*

Two forces act on a lever. One force, sometimes called the power, is applied to oppose a second force, the load. The portion of the lever between the fulcrum and the applied force is called the *power arm.* The portion between the fulcrum and the load is the *load arm.* The *mechanical advantage* of a lever depends upon the relationship between its two arms. If the power arm is longer, the mechanical advantage is greater than one. The applied force, then, will counterbalance a load larger than itself. Energy is not created by such a lever, however, for the smaller force must move through a correspondingly greater distance than the larger one. If the load arm is longer, the mechanical advantage is less than one. The applied force must be larger than the load in order to balance or move it. In this case, the lever multiplies speed at the expense of force. A large, slow-moving force applied near the fulcrum can cause a smaller load farther removed from the fulcrum to move more rapidly. This principle is used in the catapult.

If the arms are of equal length, the applied force will balance a load of equal magnitude. The only use for such a lever is to change the direction of a force. A lever or other machine in which a one-pound applied force can balance a five-pound load has a mechanical advantage of five. In a lever for which friction can be neglected, the mechanical advantage is also equal to the length of the power arm divided by the length of the load arm.

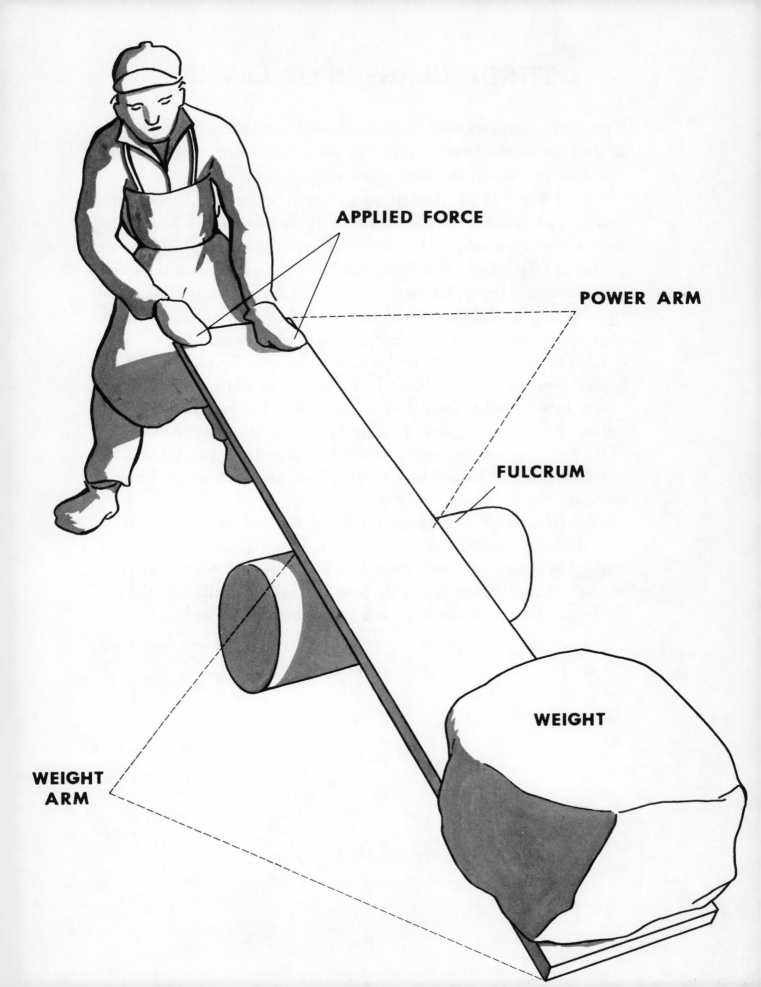

APPLIED FORCE

POWER ARM

FULCRUM

WEIGHT

WEIGHT ARM

THREE CLASSES OF LEVERS

THE LEVER is an extremely simple machine. But we can vary the location of the fulcrum of a lever in relation to the applied force and load. These variations give rise to the three classes of levers.

Class I levers. When the fulcrum is located between the applied force and the load, the lever is a first-class lever. If the power arm is longer than the load arm, a lever of this class can be used to increase force. If the reverse is true, and the power arm is the shorter, the lever will increase the speed. The direction of the applied force is always reversed, so that the load moves up when the applied force moves down. A see-saw is a lever of the first class. Other examples are scissors, balances, crowbars, and oars.

Class II levers. When the load is situated between the fulcrum and the applied force, the lever is a second-class lever. Because the applied force is always located farther from the fulcrum than is the load, a lever of the second class always magnifies force at the expense of speed. The direction of the force remains unchanged. Wheelbarrows and two-wheeled carts are second-class levers. Nutcrackers, bottle openers, and doors are also levers of this class.

Class III levers. When the applied force is between the fulcrum and the load, the lever is a third-class lever. There is always a gain in speed and a consequent loss in force with a third-class lever, because the applied force is nearer to the fulcrum than is the load. Baseball bats, golf clubs, shovels, the human mouth, mouse traps, and grass shears are all third-class levers.

Photos: Meisel from Monkmeyer; Ewing Galloway

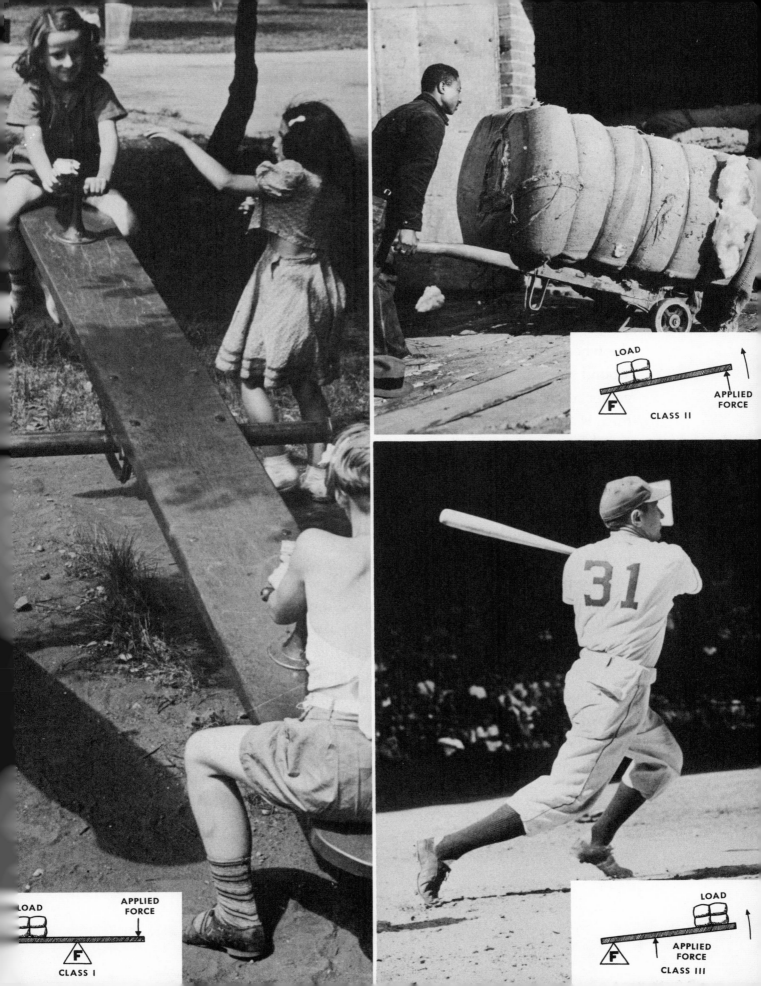

LOAD

APPLIED FORCE

CLASS II

LOAD

APPLIED FORCE

CLASS I

LOAD

APPLIED FORCE

CLASS III

THE PRINCIPLE OF THE
WHEEL AND AXLE

THE DEVICE we call the wheel and axle consists of a wheel with a shaft—the axle—attached perpendicularly at its center. The diameter of the axle is smaller than that of the wheel. In some instances, as in the differential pulley, the axle is tremendously shortened and actually becomes a small wheel securely fixed to a larger one. The wheel itself may be modified by removing all of its body except a portion along one radius. In this case, we call the device a crank.

In use, a rope or cable is often attached to and wound around the rim of the wheel. Another rope is fixed to, and wound in the opposite direction around the axle. Because the wheel and axle are securely fastened together, each time the wheel is turned the axle also turns. Thus, when a force is applied to the wheel's rope the load which is secured to the axle's rope is raised.

If we picture the radius of the wheel and that of the axle as being continuous, we notice that the principle of the wheel and axle is the same as the principle of the first-class lever. The radius of the wheel is like the power arm of the lever. The radius of the axle can be thought of as the load arm of the lever. The common center of the wheel and axle then becomes the fulcrum. The mechanical advantage of the wheel and axle, therefore, is equal to the length of the radius of the wheel (power arm) divided by the length of the radius of the axle (load arm).

When a force is applied to the wheel, the power arm is longer than the load arm. The mechanical advantage is greater than one and the machine magnifies force at the sacrifice of speed. On the other hand, if the force is applied to the axle, the shorter arm of the imaginary lever is the power arm. The mechanical advantage, then, is less than one and the machine is used to increase speed at the expense of force.

Photo: David L. Hunsberger from F.P.G.

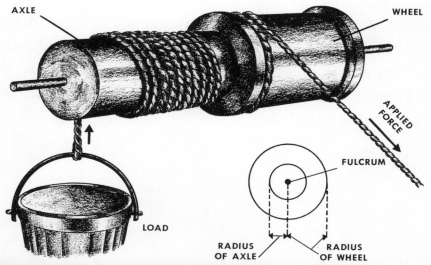

AXLE

WHEEL

APPLIED FORCE

FULCRUM

LOAD

RADIUS OF AXLE

RADIUS OF WHEEL

APPLICATIONS OF THE WHEEL AND AXLE

THE WHEEL AND AXLE can be used to change the magnitude of a force, to change its speed, to change the direction of its motion, or to transmit a force from one place to another or from one object to another.

A few common wheel and axle devices are: doorknobs, egg beaters, clothes wringers, screw drivers, clockworks, hand drills, and telephone dials. In some of these, the wheel (perhaps the axle, too) is toothed to form a gear. Gears which fit together or mesh have teeth of the same size. The relative speed of meshing gears and their mechanical advantage, therefore, depends upon the ratio between the number of teeth on the gears. For example, a gear with five teeth will move twice as rapidly as one with ten teeth that is meshed with it and the system will double a force applied to the smaller gear.

There are several basic types of gears. The most common kind is the *spur gear*. The surfaces of its teeth are parallel to the axle. The teeth of a *bevel gear* are at an angle to the axle. Bevel gears are used to change the axis of the force.

A *worm gear* consists of a short, revolving screw (the worm) whose threads mesh with the teeth of a spur gear (worm wheel). Such gearing is used to transmit a force where two axles cross at right angles, but in different planes. By use of the screw, the mechanical advantage of the gear is made extraordinarily large. Such a gear is used in the steering mechanism of an automobile.

Internal gearing allows the power gear and the load gear to rotate in the same direction. The smaller gear is a normal spur gear and the larger one is a hollow rim toothed on its inner side.

If the hollow gear of an internal gear were split and flattened, the device would be a *rack and pinion*. This combination converts the rotary motion of a spur gear to longitudinal motion in a movable toothed bar, the rack. A printer's proof press uses a rack and pinion. In this case, the pinion moves and the rack is stationary.

Photo: courtesy Elgin Watch Co.

142

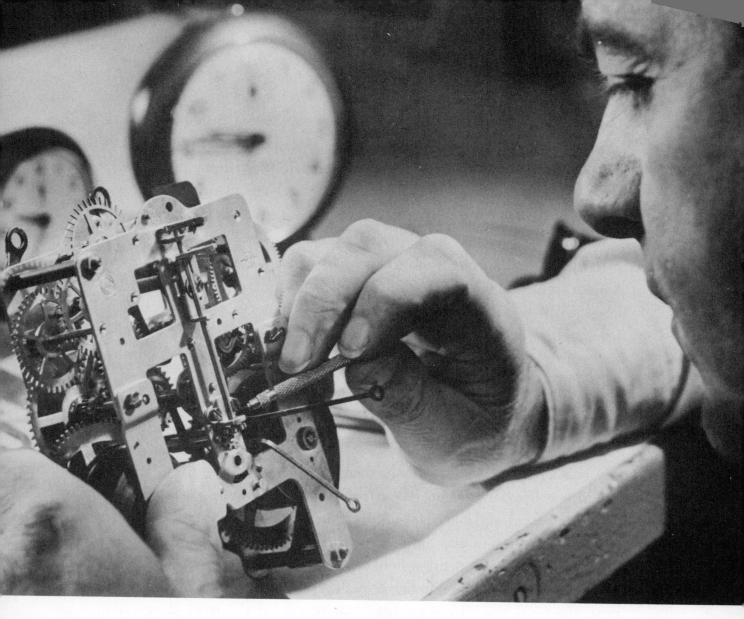

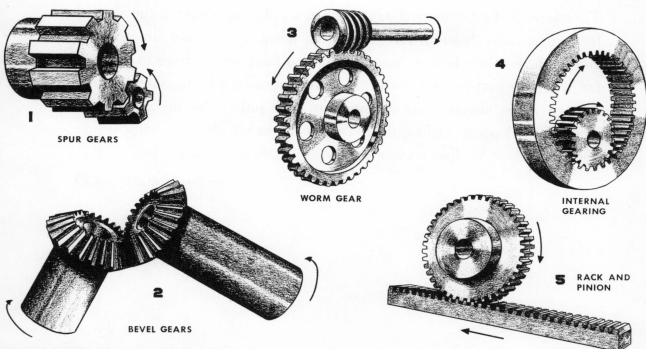

1 SPUR GEARS

2 BEVEL GEARS

3 WORM GEAR

4 INTERNAL GEARING

5 RACK AND PINION

THE PULLEY

A WHEEL, an axle, and a frame are the components of a simple machine known as the pulley. The wheel and axle of the pulley are not rigidly joined together as in the wheel and axle machine. Instead, the wheel is free to spin on the axle. The axle and the wheel are mounted in a rigid frame called a block. A rope or flexible chain is fitted into the grooved rim of the wheel, or sheave, to prepare the pulley for use.

If the pulley is hung from a stationary object, it is said to be fixed. A force applied to one end of the rope in a single, fixed pulley will balance a weight of equal magnitude hung on the other end. The mechanical advantage of such a machine, therefore, is one. It can magnify neither force nor speed. Its only virtue is that it conveniently allows a downward pull to lift a load.

If the load is hung directly on the pulley and one end of the rope is attached to a fixed object, the pulley is movable. A force applied to the free end of the rope will balance a load twice as large. The mechanical advantage of a single movable pulley is, therefore, two.

The mechanical advantage of a pulley system can be made large by combining fixed and movable pulleys. The theoretical mechanical advantage of a system with one continuous rope is equal to the number of rope segments which support the weight.

Two factors limit the number of pulleys which can be used in a system. First, the work done by a machine cannot exceed the work done on it. Therefore, if the mechanical advantage of a pulley system is 2, the applied force must move twice as far as the load; when it is 4, four times as far, and so on. For very large values, the applied force would have to move so far to lift the load that the use of the pulley would not be feasible. Second, there is a considerable loss of energy in each pulley due to friction (see page 154). A point might quickly be reached at which more work would need to be done to offset friction in the pulleys than to lift the load.

Photo: Standard Oil Co. (N.J.)

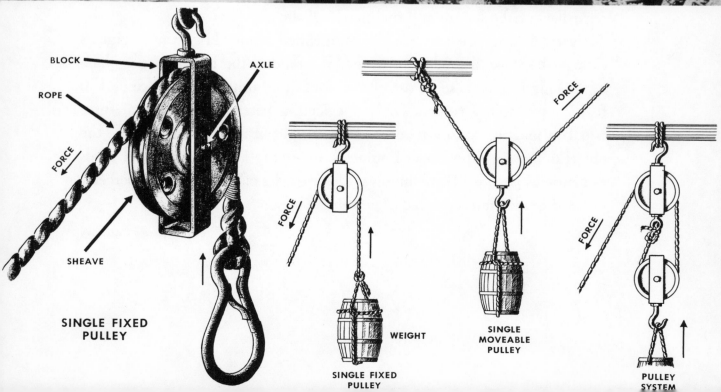

BLOCK

AXLE

ROPE

FORCE

SHEAVE

SINGLE FIXED PULLEY

FORCE

WEIGHT

SINGLE FIXED PULLEY

FORCE

SINGLE MOVEABLE PULLEY

FORCE

PULLEY SYSTEM

THE INCLINED PLANE

HILLSIDES, stairways, mountain roads, ramps, and chutes are all inclined planes. An inclined plane is merely a straight, sloping surface. It is stationary and without moving parts. This simple machine is used to raise heavy objects more easily than by lifting them vertically.

A horizontal plane, such as the floor of your home, supports the entire weight of an object placed upon it. A vertical plane, such as a wall, supports no part of the weight of an object placed against it. Inclined planes are intermediate between these extremes. They support a portion of the object's weight. A plane that forms a low angle with the horizon will support a greater portion of the weight of an object than will a steeper plane.

To cause an object to move up an inclined plane, you must exert a force slightly greater than the unsupported portion of the weight of the object. The gentler the slope of the plane, therefore, the smaller is the effort required to move an object, but the longer the plane must be to reach a given height. Conversely, a greater force is required to move an object up a steeper plane, but the plane need not be so long.

Neglecting friction, the mechanical advantage of an inclined plane is equal to the length of the plane divided by its height. The longer the plane, the greater will be its mechanical advantage. However, the total amount of work required to raise an object to a given height is the same, regardless of the length and inclination of the plane.

Every sloping street or road is an inclined plane. Highway engineers express the slope or grade of a road as the ratio of the height of the plane to the length of its base. A rise of four feet in a horizontal distance of 100 feet is equal to a 4 percent grade. Neglecting friction, a horizontal force equal in magnitude to 4 percent of the weight of an object will cause the object to move up this slope. Engineers attempt to keep the grades of roads as gentle as possible. Some highways have grades of as much as 12 percent; railroad grades rarely exceed 2 percent.

Photo: Ewing Galloway

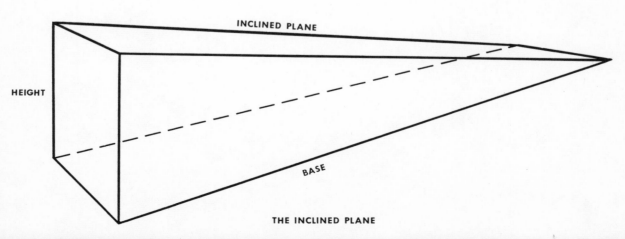

INCLINED PLANE

HEIGHT

BASE

THE INCLINED PLANE

THE WEDGE

MAN LEARNED the value of the wedge long before the dawn of civilization. The ancient inhabitants of the earth found that odd-shaped stones were useful for cutting meats, scraping animal skins, hoeing the ground, digging, and hunting wild animals. The wedge is prominent in all of our modern cutting tools, including axes, knives, chisels, wood planes, picks, plows, splitting wedges, and saw teeth. Other familiar wedges are nails, bullets, straight pins, arrowheads, and your own front teeth.

Scientists usually interpret the wedge as a modification of the inclined plane. Instead of pushing a load up the wedge or inclined plane, we push the wedge under the load. The wedge, of course, must be made of a substance harder than the object on which it is to be used.

Some wedges, such as the chisels and your front teeth, are single inclined planes. Other wedges—axe and knife blades—are composed of two inclined planes joined base to base.

Because of the enormous effort necessary to overcome the friction encountered in using a wedge, there is no simple expression for its mechanical advantage. The general principles of the inclined plane are applicable, however, to the wedge. To make the mechanical advantage of the wedge as large as possible, the angle formed at the intersection of the faces of the wedge should be as small as possible. In any case, the effort will move through a greater distance than will the resistance. If a wedge 3 inches wide and 15 inches long is used to split a log, the wedge must move 15 inches to spread the wood only 3 inches. The effort, therefore, travels 5 times as far as the resistance is moved. The wedge multiplies force at the expense of speed.

Photo: courtesy U.S. Forest Service

FACE

BASE

THE SCREW

THE SCREW is actually a well-disguised inclined plane. In the screw the plane is tightly coiled around a rigid cylinder or rod. The edge of this inclined plane is modified to form a spiral or helical ridge, called the thread. The successive turns of the thread are separated by a spiral groove whose width is uniform throughout the length of the screw. The width of this groove, measured parallel to the long axis of the screw and between the crests of two successive turns of the thread, is called the pitch of the screw.

Enormous multiplication of force is possible with the screw. This is particularly true when a lever is used to turn the screw. The theoretical mechanical advantage of this combination is equal to the distance through which the effort travels in one rotation divided by the pitch of the screw. If a 7-inch-long lever were used to turn a screw with a pitch of .04 inch, the effort would travel in a circle of 44 inches circumference. The theoretical mechanical advantage of the machine, therefore, would be 1,000. Friction usually reduces the actual mechanical advantage to a small fraction of this.

The principle of the screw is used in this brace and bit and in many other common devices, including automobile jacks, vises, faucets, swivel chairs, food grinders, jar lids, bench clamps; and, of course, wood and metal screws, and nuts and bolts.

Photo: Ewing Galloway

BOLT

HEAD

THREAD

GROOVE

PITCH

CYLINDER

INCLINED PLANE

FRIENDLY FRICTION

WITHOUT FRICTION your feet would slide out from under you as if you were continually walking on ice. This girl could not push her scooter. Nails and screws would drop out of their holes. The threads that make up a piece of cloth would slide apart. Knots and bows would not stay tied; and no object could begin to move, nor—once in motion—could it stop.

Friction is the resistance met with when one object moves over another object or through another substance. Friction always works opposite to the direction in which the object is moving, tending either to slow or stop its motion.

Rolling friction is much less than sliding friction. For example, an automobile speeds along the highways until we apply the brakes. Then, if the wheels lock, they stop rolling and friction between the tires and the road increases so much that the car skids to a stop.

Sliding friction is caused primarily by the pits and ridges of one surface interlocking with those of another surface. Friction increases as the contacting surfaces become rougher and as the force pressing the surfaces together increases.

Rolling friction is produced by two occurrences: 1) A rolling object is temporarily flattened at the point where it contacts the surface upon which it is moving. 2) The surface beneath the rolling object is pushed into a small ridge which the rolling object is perpetually forced to climb.

Friction converts mechanical energy into heat energy. In cold weather you may rub your hands together and warm them with the heat of friction. And when you strike a match, the heat of friction causes it to burst into flame.

Photo: Ewing Galloway

FRICTION, AN UNWELCOME GUEST

REGARDLESS OF THE KIND of machine, its complexity, or size, the work it does is always less than the work done on it. Friction—an unwelcome guest in every machine—is responsible for this loss of work. Engineers, therefore, are constantly working to develop new methods to reduce friction and thereby increase the efficiency of our machines.

One way to reduce friction is to make the surfaces that must rub together as smooth as possible. For example, machine parts are designed with smooth surfaces to reduce friction between them.

Rolling friction is much smaller than sliding friction. In modern machinery, therefore, balls or rollers are often inserted between an object and the surface over which it moves to convert a sliding action to a rolling one.

The discovery that friction between the layers of a liquid is much less than that between two solids has led to the development of lubricants, such as oils and greases. Lubricants are used to coat the contacting surfaces of solids. Friction then occurs partly between the layers of the liquid lubricant and partly between the solids. The lubricant further reduces friction by filling in the smaller irregularities in the contacting surfaces of the solids, and by forcing the surfaces apart slightly, thereby eliminating some of the interlocking.

In modern machines, all three methods of combating friction are employed. Surfaces are smoothed, ball and roller bearings are freely used, and all moving parts (including the ball bearings) are carefully lubricated. This picture shows a railroad worker oiling a steam locomotive.

Photo: H. Armstrong Roberts

CHAPTER VI

PHYSICS IN EVERYDAY LIFE

EVERY MODERN HOUSEHOLD is filled with appliances, tools, and complex machines which make practical use of the basic principles of matter and energy. Our highways, airlines, railroads, and factories are filled with machines which employ these basic principles.

In this chapter are shown some of the greatest inventions that our civilization has produced. Many of these inventions would have been considered impossible only a generation or two ago. Many of them may be replaced by new inventions within our generation or the next.

Photo: courtesy United Airlines

THE STEAM ENGINE

WHEN HEATED to its boiling point, water expands to form steam. This simple fact led to the development of the steam engine, the first machine that enabled men to generate power where and when it was desired. It provided a portable power source to drive railroad trains and ocean-going vessels.

The heart of the steam engine is its boiler. Here water, the lifeblood of the engine, is heated by a fire until it boils. The steam generated in the boiler passes, under high pressure, to the steam chest. From this distributing point the steam is fed through a small opening or port into a cylinder.

Upon entering the cylinder, the steam expands and pushes against a snug-fitting but movable piston. As the piston is pushed toward the end of the cylinder, a valve in the steam chest slides over the port which had admitted steam to the cylinder, thereby closing it, and at the same time opens another port. This permits steam to enter in front of the piston. The piston is then forced back to its former position, whereupon the valve again reverses the steam ports and initiates the piston cycle anew. The movement of the piston forces out the spent steam of the last stroke through the exhaust.

The piston is attached to the crankshaft by a driving rod. As the piston is pushed back and forth by the steam, it turns the crankshaft. A heavy flywheel attached to the crankshaft gains sufficient momentum from this movement to enable it to give back some energy to the piston, moving it past the "blind spots" at each end of the cylinder. Machines that are to be powered by a steam engine may be directly attached to the crankshaft or may be driven by a belt fixed to the flywheel. In the railroad locomotive, the part of the flywheel is actually played by driving wheels that propel the locomotive.

Photo: courtesy Union Pacific Railroad

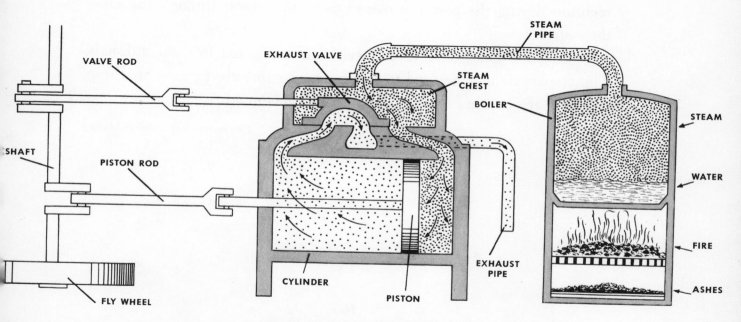

VALVE ROD

SHAFT

PISTON ROD

FLY WHEEL

EXHAUST VALVE

STEAM PIPE

STEAM CHEST

BOILER

STEAM

WATER

FIRE

ASHES

CYLINDER

PISTON

EXHAUST PIPE

DIAGRAM OF STEAM ENGINE

THE GAS ENGINE

THE UNITED STATES has more than 50 million portable chemical factories. These factories are gas engines in which oxygen is combined with a fuel, usually gasoline, producing carbon dioxide and water. But we are primarily interested in another product—power.

A gas engine is like a steam engine in that an expanding gas pushing against a piston is the source of power. It differs from a steam engine in that its fire is intermittent and occurs within the cylinder. Gas engines, therefore, are called internal combustion engines. A gas engine drives each automobile on our highways.

In most gas engines, there are four piston strokes for each fuel explosion: (1) *The intake stroke.* As the piston moves downward, a valve in the cylinder head momentarily opens to allow the fuel-air mixture to enter. (2) *The compression stroke.* The piston moves upward and compresses the mixture into the upper portion of the cylinder. (3) *The power stroke.* An electric spark, produced at the base of the spark plug, ignites the mixture. The heat of combustion causes the gaseous products, carbon dioxide and water vapor, to expand rapidly. The gases push the piston downward, turning the crankshaft to which it is attached. (4) *The exhaust stroke.* As the piston again rises, another valve in the cylinder head momentarily opens to allow the spent gases to escape through the exhaust pipe. The next stroke is a new intake stroke.

The flywheel, which is attached to the crankshaft, gains enough momentum during the power stroke to carry the piston through the other three strokes.

Most gas engines have several cylinders connected to the crankshaft. The crankshaft may be used to transfer power directly to some machine. A belt, gears, or other transfer system can also be used.

Photo: courtesy General Motors

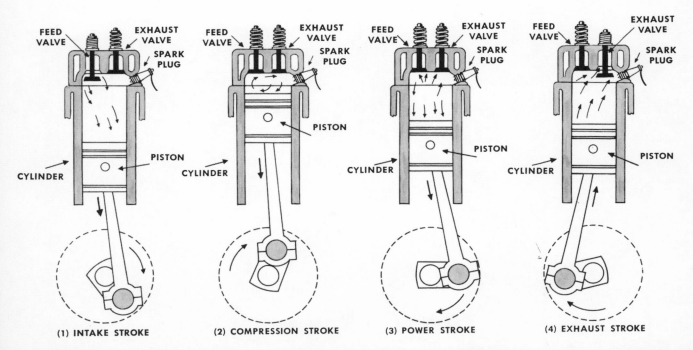

(1) INTAKE STROKE   (2) COMPRESSION STROKE   (3) POWER STROKE   (4) EXHAUST STROKE

THE DIESEL ENGINE

LARGE TRUCKS and buses, bulldozers, electric power plants, municipal water-pumping stations, railroad trains, and many other huge machines are powered by diesel engines.

The diesel, like the gas engine, is an internal combustion engine. However, it is less expensive to operate than a gas engine because it burns fuel oil rather than more highly-refined gasoline or kerosene. The design of the diesel engine is simpler than that of the gas engine because it requires neither a carburetor to mix its fuel with air, nor an electrical system to create a spark to ignite the fuel. Its chief disadvantages are that it is comparatively large and heavy in relation to the power it develops.

In operation, the diesel engine is similar to the gas engine. As the piston surges downward, air drawn into the cylinder is compressed by the return stroke of the piston. The air is crammed into about one-sixteenth of its original volume, causing its temperature to rise to about 1,000° F. Fuel oil sprayed into the cylinder then meets the hot gas and spontaneously ignites. The rapidly-expanding gases drive the piston downward, turning the crankshaft, and supplying power. Spent gases are pushed out of the cylinder as the piston rises again.

Photo: courtesy Chicago, Rock Island & Pacific Railroad

THE TURBINE

STEAM, GAS, AND DIESEL engines are reciprocating engines; that is, they depend on the alternate back-and-forth movement of a piston. At the end of each stroke the piston momentarily stops before its motion is reversed. A large portion of the energy of the fuel is used alternately to oppose the piston's inertia of motion, and then its inertia of rest. In contrast, the motion of a turbine is rotary and continuous. No energy is wasted by alternately reversing direction.

Turbines are driven by the kinetic energy of steam, heated air, or falling water. The water turbine was illustrated on page 108. Turbines driven by jets of steam turn generators which furnish electricity to many large cities. The escaping steam is directed against the blades of the turbine wheel or rotor. But the velocity of the steam is so great that its energy cannot be efficiently absorbed by a single rotor, unless the rotor were to spin at a fantastic speed. Therefore, several rotors are attached to the turbine shaft, as shown in the photograph.

Steam from several nozzles strikes the curved blades of the rotor, thereby turning it. The steam then passes through the rotor to a set of stationary blades. These blades are curved so that the steam is directed against the next rotor at the proper angle. The number of rotors, usually about 26, varies according to the pressure of the steam used to drive the turbine.

Jet engines are modified gas turbines. They are similar in design to the stationary gas turbine. But stationary turbines differ in that all of the surplus kinetic energy of the hot gases is expanded against the rotors. The gases expand to normal atmospheric pressure before being allowed to escape from the engine.

Photo: courtesy Allis-Chalmers

THE ELECTRIC MOTOR

GIANT LOCOMOTIVES, huge industrial machines, and tiny electric razors are but a few of the millions of devices powered by electric motors. Regardless of size, every electric motor is designed to do one thing, to convert electrical energy to mechanical energy.

A simple electric motor has three basic parts: a rotating electromagnet (the armature), a stationary magnet, and a pair of contact strips (brushes) which carry electricity to the armature.

When an electric current surges through wires of the armature, the armature becomes an electromagnet (see page 102). When the poles of the armature are opposite like poles of the stationary magnet, the poles repel one another and the armature is forced to turn (1). As it turns, the poles are attracted by the opposite poles of the stationary magnet (2). But, just as the opposite poles of the two magnets come together, the direction of flow of electricity through the armature is reversed (3). This reverses the armature poles and brings like poles of the magnets opposite again (4), to continue the rotation.

Reversal of current is accomplished by the use of a metal ring, the commutator, which is split into two sections. Each section is connected to one end of the armature coil. As the armature rotates, each commutator section is alternately in contact with the positive and then with the negative brush. Each end, therefore, is alternately the north and then the south pole of the armature.

The intermittent reversal of poles keeps the armature and its axle continuously rotating. The mechanical energy of the rotating armature is used to drive machines connected either directly or indirectly to the axle.

Photo: courtesy Pennsylvania Railroad

1
N
N
N
S
S
+ BRUSH
BRUSH
ARMATURE

2
N
N
COMMUTATOR
TATIONARY MAGNET
STATIONARY MAGNET
S

3
N
N
S
S

4
N
N
N
S
S

THE JET ENGINE

HAVE YOU EVER WATCHED an escaped toy balloon dart swiftly about the room? If so, you have witnessed a demonstration of the fundamental law that for every action there is an equal and opposite reaction. In this case, the backward escape of air from the balloon is the action, and the forward motion of the balloon is the reaction.

Jet engines, primarily used in airplanes, are based on this reaction principle. Air is drawn into the front of the engine, compressed, and mixed with fuel. A spark then ignites the mixture, producing superheated gases which escape at a high speed from the rear of the engine. This backward rush of gas, pushing against the combustion chamber of the engine, causes the plane to speed forward.

Although they are among our most advanced machines, jets are the most simple of all engines. The ramjet, the simplest jet, is little more than a hollow tube fitted with a fuel combustion chamber. Because it has no way to draw air into itself, air must be rammed into the ramjet. This is done by launching the ramjet plane from a "mother plane" at a high speed, or by using the ramjet to supply extra power for planes already in flight.

The turbojet needs no flying start. Blades near its mouth draw in air, making outside air unnecessary. Before the hot gases produced by the combustion of the fuel are allowed to escape, they are passed through a set of turbine rotors attached to a shaft which runs through the engine. As the rotors and shaft turn, they move the blades to draw more air into the engine.

The turboprop engine is a slight modification of the turbojet. The turbine not only supplies air to the engine, but also turns a regular propeller to help power the plane.

Photo: Ewing Galloway

TURBOJET

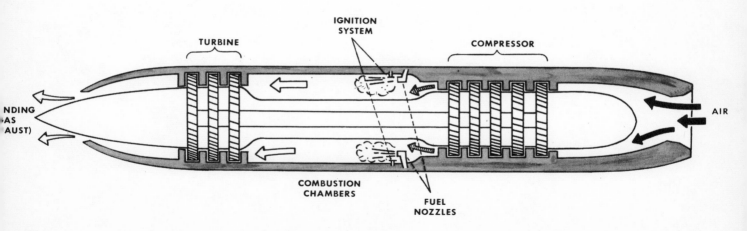

TURBINE

IGNITION SYSTEM

COMPRESSOR

NDING AS AUST)

AIR

COMBUSTION CHAMBERS

FUEL NOZZLES

ROCKETS

Like the jet, the rocket engine works on the reaction principle. It differs from the jet in that it requires no outside supply of oxygen. Rocket engines, therefore, can operate in the near-vacuum which exists at high altitudes and in space. Rocket-powered missiles have attained a maximum speed of over 6,800 miles per hour, and have risen 250 miles above the earth.

Rockets are completely self-contained. In addition to a supply of fuel, they also carry a supply of oxygen. Their oxygen may be carried separately, or it may be in a combined form in one of the fuels. Because rockets need no air, their noses are solid and not open, as are those of jet engines.

There are two basic types of rockets, depending on the fuel they use:

Solid-fuel rockets, similar to those in use as fireworks for centuries, are used for small tasks. Many are used to assist airplanes during take-offs. Others are used as auxiliary power sources for airplanes and missiles in flight. They are also widely used to supplement artillery and as armament on fighter planes.

Liquid-fuel rockets are of more recent development. They are more complex and more efficient than solid-fuel types. One type of liquid-fuel rocket uses nitric acid (HNO_3) and aniline ($C_6H_5NH_2$) as fuel. When these liquids are mixed, a violent chemical reaction releases a tremendous volume of hot gases. These gases propel the rocket.

The life of a rocket engine is very short. Solid-fuel rockets rarely last more than 15 seconds. Liquid-fuel types may last seven times as long. But once it is fired, a rocket engine is doomed to be consumed by the heat of the combustion of its own fuel.

Photo: courtesy Martin Co.

THE AIRPLANE

Every airplane, whether it is powered by a gas engine, jet engine, or rocket engine is acted upon by four forces—lift, thrust, gravity, and drag.

Lift. The pressure of a fluid decreases as the speed of flow of the fluid increases. This law is the basic principle of the airplane. The upper surface of the plane's wing is slightly curved. As the plane pushes forward, the air which passes over the wing is forced to travel farther and faster than the air which passes under it. Both parcels of air arrive at the back edge of the wing at the same instant. The air pressure from below, therefore, is greater than the air pressure from above. This difference causes the wing to be lifted vertically.

Thrust acts to speed the plane on its way. In cross-section an airplane propeller is shaped much like a wing. Its leading surface is curved and its back surface is flat. When the propeller is rotated by the engine, air pressure is greater against the back of the propeller than against the front. As a result, the propeller and the plane to which it is attached, are pushed forward. This forward push is the thrust. The thrust of a jet airplane is the reaction to backward-escaping gases.

Gravity. The earth's gravitational attraction works against lift, and tends to pull the plane toward the ground.

Drag tends to retard a plane's progress. Like all other matter, air has substance. An airplane must push the air aside as it moves forward. Air resistance causes a loss of forward speed. Eddy currents form in the air behind each exposed part of the airplane, causing a further resistance to forward motion. The total effect of air resistance at the front, and of eddies at the back of each exposed part constitutes the drag.

When a plane is in level flight and traveling at a constant speed, the four forces are in balance—lift equals gravity, and thrust equals drag.

LIFT

DRAG

THRUST

GRAVITY

THE TELEPHONE

FOR BUSINESS, for pleasure, in emergencies—the telephone is used 190 million times a day throughout the United States. Let us see what makes a telephone work.

The transmitter is the part of the instrument into which you speak. Sound waves from your voice cause a thin metal diaphragm in the transmitter to vibrate. These vibrations are carried to a small box of carbon granules located behind the diaphragm. If your telephone is off the hook, an electrical current is continuously flowing through this carbon. When a vibration squeezes the box, the carbon granules are pushed more tightly together, permitting a stronger current to pass through them. In this way, a varying electrical current whose pulsations correspond to the vibrations caused by your voice, is sent out from the transmitter.

The pulsating electrical current is carried over wires, through a central telephone office, and finally to another telephone. There, in the receiver (the part of the instrument that you hold against your ear) the current passes into wires coiled around a small magnet. In front of this magnet is a thin iron diaphragm. When an electric current flows through the wire coils, the magnet becomes stronger and pulls the diaphragm toward it. As the current ebbs, the diaphragm snaps away again.

The motion of the diaphragm in the receiver duplicates that of the diaphragm in the transmitter. The receiver, therefore, produces sound waves similar to those you produced by speaking. When these waves strike the ear of the person at the other end of the line, he hears your words.

Photos: Ewing Galloway; A.T.&T.

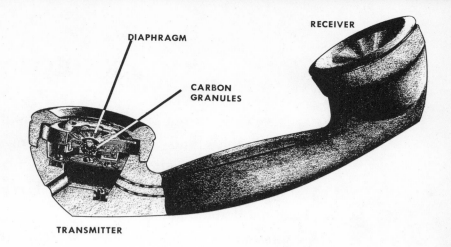

DIAPHRAGM

CARBON
GRANULES

RECEIVER

TRANSMITTER

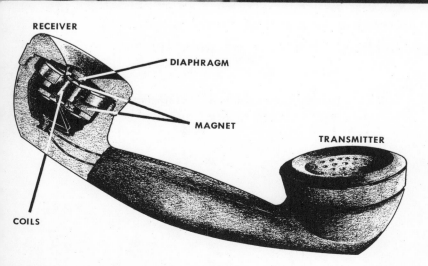

RECEIVER

DIAPHRAGM

MAGNET

TRANSMITTER

COILS

RADIO

When an announcer speaks into a microphone (a type of telephone transmitter), the sound of his voice is changed to a fluctuating electric current. This current is used to shape or modulate a uniform series of high-frequency electromagnetic carrier waves. The modulated waves are broadcast from a tall antenna.

An alternating current is induced in the antenna or circuits of your radio set by waves broadcast from the station. In the radio set, this current is strengthened and changed to a fluctuating direct current. It then flows to an electromagnet in the loudspeaker. As the electromagnet alternately strengthens and weakens, it causes a diaphragm to vibrate, converting the electric current back to sound waves.

Radio circuits employ a number of vacuum tubes. When a piece of metal is heated in a vacuum, electrons "boil off." If a positively-charged metallic plate is introduced near the heated metal, the electrons flow toward it. A *diode* is a vacuum tube which contains a plate and a metal filament that can be heated by an electric current. These tubes can change an alternating current to direct current, because electrons will flow from the filament to the plate, but not in the opposite direction.

In a *triode,* a metallic screen or grid is inserted between the filament and plate, as shown in the diagram. The stream of electrons will pass readily through the uncharged grid. If the grid is negatively charged, the electrons will be repelled. The flow can be increased by placing a positive charge on the grid. Thus, if the weak current from the antenna is fed to the grid and allowed to modify the current from the filament, the current which reaches the plate will be similar to, but stronger than the original antenna current. The current from the plate of one tube can be fed to the grid of another and further strengthened. This process can be repeated several times. In this way, very weak signals are amplified until they are strong enough to operate the loud speaker.

Photo: courtesy Columbia Broadcasting System

FILAMENT
GLASS COVER
PLATE
PLATE
GRID
FILAMENT

TELEVISION

ACTION IN A TELEVISION studio is "photographed" by a special kind of camera. In this camera, an image of the scene is focused on a metal plate rather than on film. The plate, the screen of an electronic tube, is covered with flecks of cesium. This metal releases electrons when it is exposed to light. A fleck, upon which a bright portion of the image falls, releases many electrons. A fleck receiving less light emits fewer electrons.

The electrons released by the cesium flow to the target, a metal plate behind the screen, where they produce variations in its normally-uniform positive charge. The original light image is changed to a pattern of strong charges corresponding to dark areas, and weak charges corresponding to lighter areas.

Only a scramble would result if the entire electric pattern were transmitted simultaneously. Therefore, before it is dispatched, the pattern is systematically divided by scanning it with a pinpoint beam of electrons from an "electron gun" at the rear of the tube. The beam is moved back and forth across each of 525 lines on the target 30 times a second. Areas with a strong positive charge absorb many electrons. Those with weak positive charges reflect many electrons. The picture consequently is changed to a fluctuating electric current which is used to modulate the carrier wave sent out by the station.

The carrier waves induce a current in the antenna of your television set. This current is amplified and it finally enters the picture tube of the set where it controls the flow of electrons from an electron gun. As the electron beam sweeps back and forth across the screen of the picture tube, it causes a fluorescent substance on the screen to glow. The intensity of light depends upon the number of electrons which strike a given point. The screen's 525 lines are scanned so quickly that the entire picture seems to be illuminated at once. The image seems to move because the picture changes thirty times each second, just as a series of still pictures projected in rapid succession on a screen give the impression of motion.

Photo: Wagner from Monkmeyer

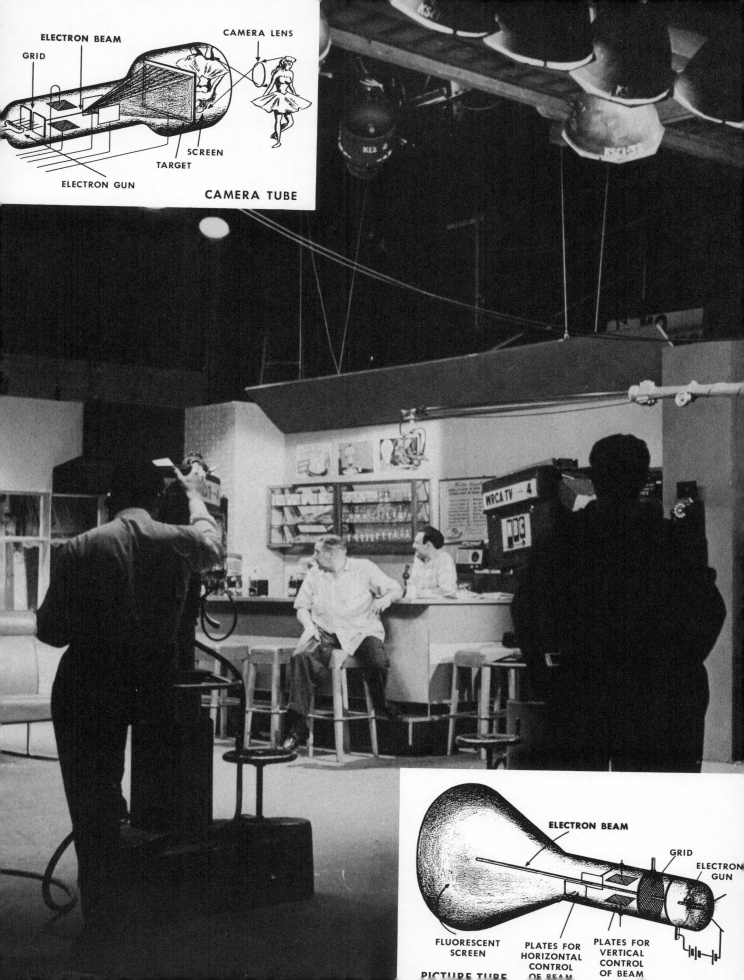

CAMERA LENS

ELECTRON BEAM

GRID

SCREEN

TARGET

ELECTRON GUN

CAMERA TUBE

ELECTRON BEAM

GRID

ELECTRON GUN

FLUORESCENT SCREEN

PLATES FOR HORIZONTAL CONTROL OF BEAM

PLATES FOR VERTICAL CONTROL OF BEAM

PICTURE TUBE

REFRIGERATION

Temperature is made to order by your refrigerator, freezer, and room air-conditioner. The same fundamental principles underlie the operation of each of these devices. An evaporating liquid absorbs heat from its surroundings, and heat may be transferred from one body or place to another. The working parts of the three devices are also similar.

In an electric refrigerator, a compressor driven by a small motor subjects a gaseous refrigerant, sulfur dioxide (SO_2), freon (CCl_2F_2) or methyl chloride (CH_3Cl), to high pressure. The compressed refrigerant then passes into thin metal condenser coils where, after losing heat to the surrounding air, it liquefies. These coils are usually mounted on the back of refrigerators and freezers. They are the outermost element in a window-type air-conditioner.

The liquid refrigerant next flows into evaporator coils. These surround the freezing compartment of your refrigerator, and are built into the shelves of a freezer. In an air-conditioner they are covered by vanes and placed just behind the grill. In these coils, the pressure is reduced and the refrigerant is allowed to expand into a gas. As this change occurs, the refrigerant absorbs heat from the coils. In turn, the coils absorb heat from the air around them. The cooled air, which is more dense than the warmer air around it, settles to the lower portion of the box. The food in the refrigerator or freezer is chilled when it loses heat to the air or directly to the metal coils. In the air-conditioner, air is chilled when it is blown across the coils by a fan. The refrigerant passes from the evaporator coils back to the compressor where it begins its journey again.

Photo: courtesy Westinghouse

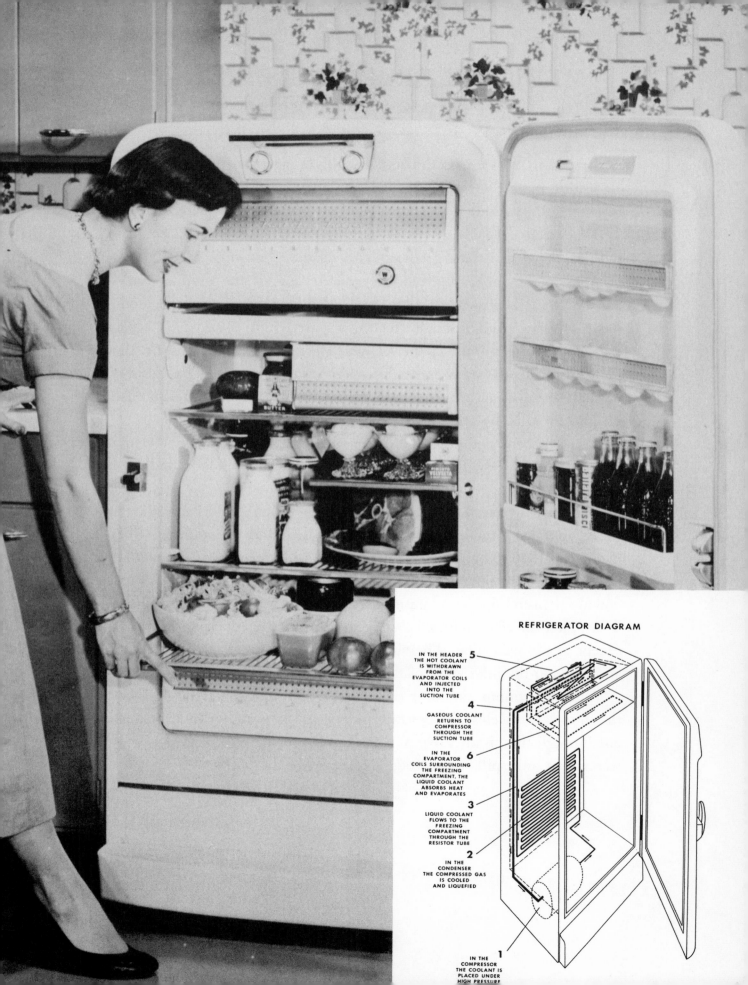

REFRIGERATOR DIAGRAM

5 — IN THE HEADER THE HOT COOLANT IS WITHDRAWN FROM THE EVAPORATOR COILS AND INJECTED INTO THE SUCTION TUBE

4 — GASEOUS COOLANT RETURNS TO COMPRESSOR THROUGH THE SUCTION TUBE

6 — IN THE EVAPORATOR COILS SURROUNDING THE FREEZING COMPARTMENT, THE LIQUID COOLANT ABSORBS HEAT AND EVAPORATES

3 — LIQUID COOLANT FLOWS TO THE FREEZING COMPARTMENT THROUGH THE RESISTOR TUBE

2 — IN THE CONDENSER THE COMPRESSED GAS IS COOLED AND LIQUEFIED

1 — IN THE COMPRESSOR THE COOLANT IS PLACED UNDER HIGH PRESSURE

MEDICINE DROPPERS, DRINKING STRAWS, AND PUMPS

A NUMBER OF DEVICES utilize atmospheric pressure—the weight of the air resting upon the earth's surface—to do work. At sea level this pressure is about 14.7 pounds per square inch or 1.07 tons per square foot.

A medicine dropper is perhaps the simplest of such devices. To operate the dropper, you submerge the mouth of the glass tube in a liquid. A squeeze on the rubber bulb at the opposite end of the dropper forces a portion of the air from the empty bulb. When released, the bulb tends to flex back to its original shape, creating a space within itself with a capacity greater than the volume of the air which it still contains. This air, therefore, must expand and so exerts less than normal pressure. The liquid is at normal pressure except near the mouth of the tube. As a result, it is pushed up into the tube by atmospheric pressure.

Fountain pens and rubber syringes operate in the same way. When you use a drinking straw, your mouth takes the place of the rubber bulb of the dropper.

Hand-operated water pumps, once a common household fixture, are still found in some rural areas. These pumps are more complicated than a medicine dropper, but they operate on the same principle. The workings of a standard pump are shown in the diagram. As the handle is pushed down, the piston inside the pump rises, creating a partial vacuum below it. The water in the ground is subjected to normal atmospheric pressure, except at the well pipe. Therefore, the water is pushed up into the pipe and through the inlet valve of the pump.

When the pump handle is raised, the piston moves downward, forcing the inlet valve to close. The water trapped in the pump cylinder is pushed out through the piston valve. On the next upward stroke of the piston, the water rises and spills out through the spout of the pump.

Photo: courtesy Standard Oil Co. (N.J.)

Piston Valve

Piston

Inlet Valve

Air Pressure

1   2   3   4   5   6

A LIFT PUMP PRODUCES UNBALANCED AIR PRESSURE

MICROSCOPES AND TELESCOPES

LENSES HAVE EXTENDED man's vision into the infinitesimally small world of the microbe, as well as to the infinitely large world of outer space. The microscope is the tool which has allowed scientists to probe the realm of the minute. The telescope has allowed them to investigate the mysteries of the distant.

A microscope contains at least two converging lenses (see page 94). The lens nearest the object to be viewed is the *objective lens*. It has a very short focal length. The other lens, into which you look, is called the *ocular lens* or *eyepiece*. It is a lens of intermediate focal length.

When an object is placed beneath the objective lens, an inverted real image, larger than the object, is formed inside the microscope. The ocular lens then forms an enlarged, virtual image of the real image. This virtual image seems to be outside and below the microscope, and is still inverted with respect to the object. Finally, the eye of the viewer transforms the virtual image to a real image on the retina (see page 94).

The simple sky telescope, like the microscope, contains two converging lenses. In the telescope, however, the objective is a lens of long focal length, while the ocular lens has a short focal length. The two lenses are separated by distance slightly less than their combined focal lengths. At this distance the inverted, real image of the distant object is formed by the objective lens inside of the focal point of the ocular lens. The ocular lens then produces an enlarged virtual image of the object, still inverted.

Even though an inverted image does not distract one gazing at a star, it would be very confusing to a person observing the movement of a ship or other object here on earth. Spyglasses, or terrestrial telescopes, therefore employ a third lens between the objective and the ocular lenses to re-invert the real image before it is enlarged by the eyepiece. Terrestrial telescopes are extensively used by land surveyors, military men, seamen, and others.

Photos: U.S. Forest Service; Ewing Galloway

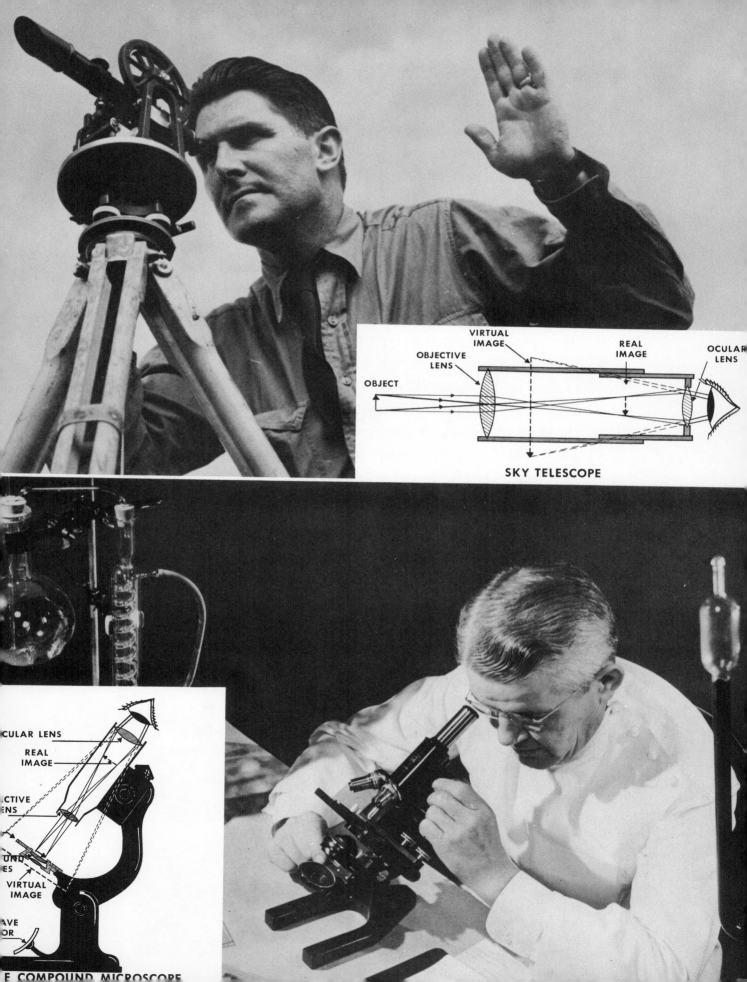

VIRTUAL IMAGE

OBJECTIVE LENS

REAL IMAGE

OCULAR LENS

OBJECT

SKY TELESCOPE

CULAR LENS

REAL IMAGE

CTIVE ENS

UND ES

VIRTUAL IMAGE

AVE OR

E COMPOUND MICROSCOPE

ELECTROLYSIS AND ELECTROPLATING

THESE BRASS FORKS are being coated with a thin plate of silver which will protect and beautify them. Many other items, such as pieces of jewelry, automobile bumpers, and electrical appliances may also be plated with silver, chromium, or some other metal. This plating is deposited from a liquid solution by an electric current.

Only solutions which contain positively and negatively-charged ions (see page 100) will conduct electricity. Such solutions, usually water solutions of an acid, base or salt, are called *electrolytes*. The passage of an electric current through an electrolyte is accompanied by a series of chemical reactions collectively known as *electrolysis*.

The electrolyte used in plating is a solution of a salt of the plate metal. In silver plating, for example, it is a solution of potassium argentous cyanide ($KAg(CN)_2$) which dissociates into potassium, silver, and cyanide ions. Thin blocks of silver, which are submerged in the solution, are connected to a battery or other source of direct-current electricity and become positive electrodes (anodes). The pieces to be plated are connected to the negative pole of the battery and become negative electrodes (cathodes). The entire unit—solution, container, and electrodes—is called an *electrolytic cell*.

Electricity enters the cell through the silver blocks and passes out through the forks. Positively-charged potassium and silver ions migrate to the forks (negative electrodes) where the silver ions are neutralized and the metal is deposited in a thin, even coating. The potassium, due to its greater resistance to de-ionization, remains in solution.

Photo: Ewing Galloway

CHAPTER VII

CHEMISTRY IN EVERYDAY LIFE

THE ALCHEMISTS of medieval times attempted to combine substances without understanding the reactions which occurred. They sought to create potions that would prolong life, or to transform common metals to precious gold and silver. They worked in scientific darkness and failed to comprehend the fundamental laws of chemistry.

Modern chemists bear slight resemblance to the alchemists of old. Modern chemists work in well-ordered laboratories, stocked with purified chemicals, and equipped with complicated apparatuses.

In these pages are some of the modern miracles they have accomplished, illustrations from the vast industries built on their discoveries—iron, steel, aluminum, petroleum, plastics. Even now, the findings of some unknown scientist may be destined to give rise to tomorrow's greatest industry or most powerful medicine.

Photo: Ewing Galloway

THE CHEMISTRY OF IRON AND STEEL

EACH YEAR over 100 millions tons of iron and steel are used by American industries. These metals are manufactured into home appliances, automobiles, food containers, ships, and trains, and are used in the construction of bridges, buildings, and reinforced highways.

Hematite (Fe_2O_3) and limonite ($2Fe_2O_3 . 3H_2O$) are the most important sources of iron. Our supply of these ores is obtained chiefly from the Mesabi Range in Minnesota. After excavation, the ore is shipped to steel-producing centers, such as Chicago, Cleveland, Detroit, and Pittsburgh.

At the steel mill, the ore is mixed with coke and limestone ($CaCO_3$), and fed into tall blast furnaces like those shown in the upper photograph. As the mixture settles through the furnace, at least 20 chemical reactions occur at various temperatures. The most important are the several reduction reactions by which carbon (coke) separates oxygen from the iron. For every ton of pig iron, the furnace also produces 2,050 pounds of slag ($CaSiO_3$) and 160,000 cubic feet of gas (CO, CO_2, N_2). The gas is used in the four stoves next to each furnace to preheat air for the furnace.

Pig iron contains from six to eight percent of impurities. It may be used directly for cast iron and wrought iron, or it may be further purified and used for steel.

About 90 percent of all American steel is produced by the open-hearth process. This steel is of great purity and is used to make machinery, girders, rails, armament, and other products. The hearth, which is about the size of a private swimming pool, is contained within a large furnace, like the one shown in the lower photograph. A charge, consisting of about 100 tons of scrap iron, limestone, iron ore, and molten pig iron is heated in the hearth for about 10 hours. During this time, impurities are removed by various chemical reactions. Exact amounts of carbon and other elements are added to the molten iron to produce steel of the quality and properties desired.

Photos: courtesy American Iron & Steel Institute

THE CHEMISTRY OF ALUMINUM

ALUMINUM PRODUCTS are all around you: in airplanes, trucks, trains, toothpaste tubes, metal foil, and many other things. But a century ago, aluminum was so precious that Emperor Napoleon III of France set aluminum utensils only before his most honored guests. The fantastic change in aluminum prices was brought about by the development, in 1886, of the relatively inexpensive Hall process for refining the metal from its ores.

Aluminum occurs in compounds with other elements, primarily oxygen. Bauxite, the most important ore, contains about 60 percent alumina (Al_2O_3), 30 percent water and 10 percent silicon dioxide (SiO_2).

The Hall process requires pure aluminum. Purification is accomplished by crushing the bauxite ore with pneumatic drills (shown here) and heating the finely divided bauxite in a solution of sodium hydroxide (NaOH). After a series of reactions, the impurities settle out, leaving aluminum hydroxide ($Al(OH)3$) as a residue. The aluminum hydroxide is then heated to change it to alumina, a white powder which resembles granulated sugar.

The alumina is dissolved in molten cryolite (Na_3AlF_6). The solution is made in a large steel tank like the one shown here. A strong current of electricity is fed into large carbon blocks suspended in the solution. The current passes through the solution to the carbon lining of the tank, making the tank an electrolytic cell. The electricity decomposes the alumina to aluminum and oxygen ions. Aluminum settles to the bottom of the tank. The oxygen ions migrate to the carbon blocks, where they combine with carbon to form carbon dioxide gas.

Molten pig aluminum is cast into molds. Later, the pig metal is remelted and the remaining impurities are skimmed off. If the aluminum is to be alloyed to modify its characteristics, other elements are added to it during the remelting step. Finally, the aluminum may be made into tubes, ingots, or thin sheets rolled on spools, such as those shown in the lower picture.

Photos: courtesy Reynolds Metal Co.

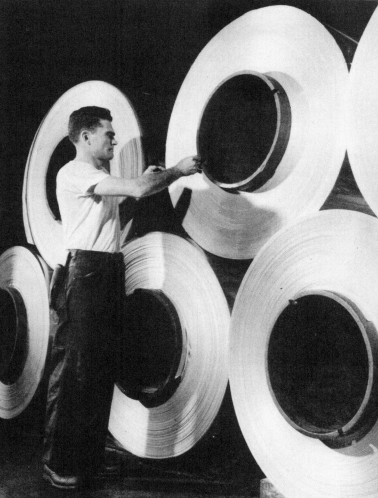

THE CHEMISTRY OF PETROLEUM

PETROLEUM, the "black gold" that gushes from oil wells throughout the world, is a mixture of hydrocarbons, compounds of carbon and hydrogen. From the oil field the petroleum is transported to the refinery, where impurities are removed by a series of chemical treatments and the various hydrocarbons are separated by physical processes.

Closely related hydrocarbons, called petroleum fractions, have very similar boiling points. This characteristic is used to separate the hydrocarbons by a process called fractional distillation. After petroleum has been heated to about 300° C. (572° F.), it is pumped into a 100-foot-tall fractioning tower, seen at the left of the photograph. Heavy oils, which do not boil at this temperature, flow immediately to the bottom of the tower. They may contain lubricating oils, paraffin or asphalt, depending upon the source of the petroleum. The remaining hydrocarbons, all vaporized, gradually cool as they rise through the tower. Gasoline liquefies first; then kerosene liquefies at a slightly higher level; then naphtha.

Each fraction is caught as it liquefies, and is led off through a complicated system of pipes to huge tanks where it is stored temporarily. The gaseous fraction which contains gasoline vapor is led off through a tube at the top of the tower. The gasoline is subsequently liquefied when the gas is cooled. The remaining portion of the fraction, a gas at normal pressure, is compressed and sold as "bottled gas" which is widely used for cooking.

Gasoline is not a single compound, but a mixture of several hydrocarbons, including hexane (C_6H_{14}), heptane (C_7H_{16}), and octane (C_8H_{18}). Due to its widespread use as a fuel for engines, gasoline is one of the most important petroleum products. Chemists, therefore, have developed methods to produce additional gasoline molecules by linking together several molecules of simpler hydrocarbons (polymerization) and by splitting up the more complex molecules of heavy oils and gas oils (cracking). The large tower in the center of the photograph is a cracking tower.

Photo: courtesy Standard Oil Co. (N.J.)

PLASTICS

POLYETHYLENE is rapidly becoming the most popular plastic. You may have several squeeze-bottles made of this material in your kitchen, workshop, or medicine cabinet. The plastic is also made into transparent bags, weather balloons, toys, electrical insulation, garden hose, irrigation pipe, and a thousand other items.

Like all synthetic plastics, polyethylene is produced by polymerization, that is, by causing small organic molecules to join together into long chains or complex networks. In its production, molecules of ethylene gas ($H_2C = CH_2$) are linked together to form seemingly endless polyethylene chains ($..CH_2CH_2CH_2CH_2...$).

A plastic is a resinous organic compound which can be molded or cast into any shape by the application of moderate heat or pressure, or both, and which will maintain this shape after cooling. Certain natural resins, such as pitch, rosin, and shellac are considered to be plastics under this restricted definition. But the great majority of plastics—more than 5,000 kinds—are synthetic substances developed in the chemical laboratory. Some of the best known are cellulose plastics, bakelite, saran, vinylite, lucite, polystyrene.

There are two general classes of plastic resins, thermosetting and thermoplastic. Thermoplastic materials can be repeatedly softened by heat and remolded to the desired shape. Thermosetting materials can be softened during the original casting, but cannot be resoftened after cooling. Chemists suspect that the molecular structure of the materials is responsible for the differences in their behavior. Thermoplastic resins, such as lucite and polyethylene, are composed of long-chain molecules with few side linkages. Molecules with numerous side linkages, in the form of complex networks, are characteristic of thermosetting resins, such as bakelite.

Photos: courtesy U.S. Air Force; Union Carbide

GLASS

LIME GLASS is the trade name of the substance from which windows, bottles, light bulbs, tableware, and a host of other inexpensive products are made. It is manufactured by heating sodium carbonate (Na_2CO_3), calcium carbonate ($CaCO_3$), and silicon dioxide (SiO_2) together. A reaction occurs which produces a lime glass ($Na_2) \cdot CaO \cdot 6SiO_2$) and carbon dioxide gas.

Glass is hard, and transparent or translucent; but it lacks a crystalline structure and does not have a definite melting point. Glass, then, cannot be a true solid. Its properties are those of an extremely viscous, or super-cooled liquid. And glass is not a compound but a mixture, because its composition can be varied through a considerable range. More than 50,000 different formulas are used to produce glasses that possess greatly diverse characteristics.

Silicon dioxide and sodium carbonate are used to manufacture all kinds of glass. Other chemicals are added to give glass special properties. Lead oxide (PbO), used in place of calcium carbonate, produces lead glass, which is more difficult to melt and shape than lime glass. Lead glass is used for radio, radar, television tubes, neon tubes, and crystal glass tableware.

Boric oxide (B_2O_3) and aluminum oxide (Al_2O_3) are used in the manufacture of borosilicate glass. This glass, which is extremely resistant to chemical attack and rapid temperature change, is ideal for chemical laboratory equipment, ovenware, and many industrial uses. Optical glasses are of various compositions, including all the foregoing types. They are, however, very carefully processed and must be free from imperfections.

Glass of almost any color can be made by mixing very small amounts of various metal oxides to a normal formula for clear glass. Nickel or cobalt produces purple glass; cobalt and copper, blue; copper or chromium or both, green; iron or carbon, yellow; gold, copper or selenium, red; and tin, white.

Photo: courtesy Corning Glass Works

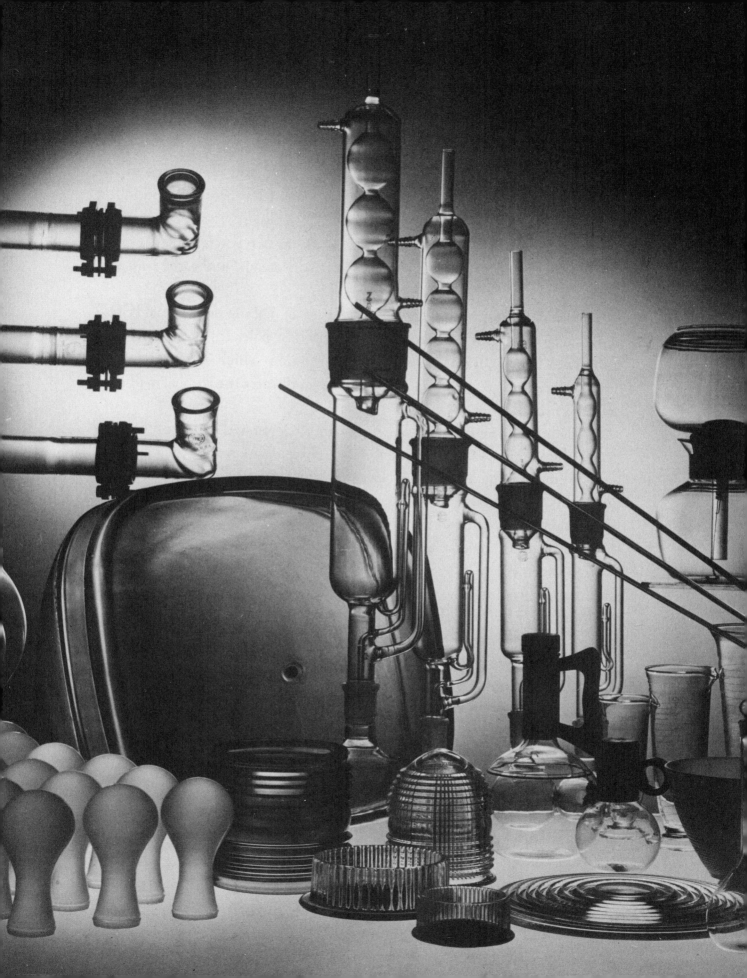

EXTINGUISHING FIRES

WHEN YOU TURN OFF your gas range you are extinguishing a fire by removing its fuel. You may have put out a camp fire by covering it with soil, thereby cutting off its oxygen. And, each time you blow out a match you are extinguishing a fire by cooling the fuel below its kindling temperature.

Water, the most familiar fire fighter, works in two ways. It blankets the fuel—shutting out oxygen—and as it changes to steam, it absorbs heat and cools the fuel.

Soda-acid extinguishers contain a solution of baking soda ($NaHCO_3$) and water. When the extinguisher is inverted, a bottleful of sulfuric acid spills into the solution, resulting in a reaction which liberates carbon dioxide. The pressure forces carbon dioxide and water through a small hose onto the fire.

In foamite extinguishers, carbon dioxide is generated by a reaction between alum ($Al_2(SO_4)_3$) and soda. As the pressure increases, the gas mixes with aluminum hydroxide ($Al(OH)_3$), a gelatinous substance also produced by the reaction, forming a foam. When sprayed over a fire, the foam, stabilized by the addition of a licorice extract, shuts out the oxygen.

Liquid carbon dioxide under high pressure is used in another kind of extinguisher. When released, part of the carbon dioxide expands into a gas, thereby cooling the other portion into solid, snow-like flakes. The expanding gas blows the snow over the fire. As it melts, the snow absorbs heat, cooling the fuel, and forms carbon dioxide gas which smothers the fire.

Pyrene extinguishers, the smallest in common use, contain pyrene or carbon tetrachloride (CCl_4). When the liquid is pumped onto a fire it boils readily, forming a heavy, non-inflammable gas that shuts off the supply of oxygen to the fuel.

Photo: courtesy National Board of Fire Underwriters

SOAP

Soap is a champion dirt chaser. It lowers the surface tension of water, thereby allowing the water to soak into the materials more readily. It greatly increases the power of water to dissolve oil and grease. It lubricates dirt particles, facilitating their removal by water. And soap acts as an emulsifier, causing substances to mix so thoroughly with water that they do not settle rapidly.

In pioneer America, soap-making was a kitchen chore. Wood ashes were soaked to secure lye ($NaOH$). When waste cooking fats ($C_3H_5(C_{17}H_{35}COO)_3$) were mixed with the lye, a slow chemical reaction took place which produced soap ($C_{17}H_{35}COONa$) and glycerine ($C_3H_5(OH)_3$).

The chemistry of soap production is virtually the same today. The small bucket on the kitchen stove, however, has given way to huge kettles which stretch up through two or three stories of a modern factory.

Soap is made by running a dilute solution of lye into a kettle filled with melted fat or oil. The mixture is heated and stirred by steam which continually bubbles through it. When the reaction is complete, in perhaps four or five days, several tons of table salt are shoveled into the kettles. Glycerine and other impurities dissolve in the brine, but the soap floats on the salty solution as a "curd." By purification, the curd is transformed to "neat." If a fine toilet soap is to be made, perfume is added to the neat.

After receiving any additives, the soap is stored in large steel boxes until it hardens. The huge soap blocks are then cut into small bars which eventually reach your grocer's shelves. Soap is also sold in the form of powders, flakes, creams, pastes, jellies, liquids, and chips.

Photo: courtesy Cleanliness Bureau

PAINT

INDIANS and other primitive people used plant juices and other natural substances for decorating themselves and their homes. Today, however, chemistry gives us an artificial rainbow of thousands of colors of paints to beautify and protect our homes, our automobiles, and a vast number of other things. Most of these paints contain three principal ingredients: pigments, binders, and thinners.

Pigments are finely-powdered solids used to impart color to the paint and to hide the surface. White lead $(2PbCO_3 \cdot Pb(OH)_2)$ is the most common paint pigment. It is inexpensive and covers well. However, it has two important disadvantages. It often makes painters ill, and it becomes gray when exposed to sulfur compounds which are often present in the air in industrialized areas. Zinc oxide, another pigment, is added to prevent this discoloration.

Shellacs and varnishes are pigment-free paints which afford protection without hiding the surface.

Binders serve to carry the pigment and to cause it to adhere to the surface being painted. Linseed oil, obtained from flax seed, is the most commonly used binder. "Plastic" paints employ as a binder a synthetic resin, such as bakelite or nylon. These binders dry, not by evaporation, but by combining with atmospheric oxygen. The oxidation reaction produces a hard, glossy film over the painted surface. Lacquers are paints which employ highly volatile organic solvents as binders. These paints, which are primarily used on automobiles, dry rapidly by evaporation.

Thinners are used to dilute the binder so that the paint can be spread easily. Once its task has been performed, the thinner evaporates, leaving only pigment and binder on the painted surface. Turpentine is the thinner most often used in paints. Water-soluble paints employ glue as a binder and water as a thinner. Evaporation of the water leaves the pigment suspended in a film of dried glue.

Photo: courtesy Paint & Varnish Production

CHEMISTRY ON THE FARM

JOHN BURKHOLDER is typical of thousands of modern farmers who use chemicals to increase the productivity of their land. On his 80-acre farm in Pennsylvania, Mr. Burkholder grows corn, hay, wheat, potatoes, and tobacco. He also raises cattle and chickens. In the course of an average year, he uses this huge mound of chemicals to fertilize or improve the soil on his farm, to supplement animal feeds, to prevent or correct plant and animal diseases, and to kill insect pests.

Fertilizers, the most important farm chemicals, are primarily used to replace elements removed from the soil by harvested crops. A tobacco crop, for example, requires approximately 166 pounds of potassium, 76 pounds of nitrogen, and 7 pounds of phosphorus from each acre. Commercial fertilizers contain these three elements in varying proportions. The choice of the fertilizer to be used on a field depends upon the requirements of the crop to be raised, and upon the condition of the soil, as revealed by chemical analyses.

About 7,000 kinds of insects are known to attack crop plants in the United States. These pests cause losses calculated in billions of dollars each year.

Chemicals used to combat insects are of three sorts: *Stomach poisons*, such as arsenic compounds $(Ca_3(AsO_4)_2)$, must be eaten to be effective. *Contact poisons*, such as pyrethrin $(C_{22}H_{30}O_5)$ and nicotine $(C_{10}H_{14}N_2)$, kill after they fall upon an insect's body. Fumigants kill after being taken into the respiratory system. Fumigants must be gases [hydrocyanic acid (HCN)], highly volatile liquids [carbon disulfide (CS_2)], or solids which sublime or change directly to the gaseous state [paradichlobenzene $(C_6H_4Cl_2)$]. Rotenone $(C_{23}H_{22}O_6)$ and dichloro-diphenyl-trichloro-ethane, better known as D.D.T. $(C_{14}H_9Cl_5)$, act as both stomach and contact poisons.

Photo: courtesy Dupont

PHOTOGRAPHY

THE FILM in your camera is a long, thin strip of cellulose acetate, a transparent plastic coated with a cream-colored suspension of silver bromide ($AgBr$) in gelatin. When you snap the camera's shutter, light strikes the film for a split second. Due to a reaction not yet completely understood, silver bromide is more easily reduced after it has been exposed to light.

When the film is developed, an alkaline solution reacts with the light-struck silver bromide to form metallic silver and a soluble compound of bromine. The blackish deposits of silver form a "pictorial memory" of the scene you photographed. In this picture, however, the bright objects of the original scene appear dark, and the dark objects appear light. Because of this reversal of tones, the picture is called a *negative*.

The action of the developer is halted by the stop bath. However, the lighter portions of the negative still contain unreduced silver bromine. To remove it, the film is placed in the fixing bath, which is an acid solution of sodium thiosulfate ($NaHS_2O_3$). The fixer reacts with the silver bromide to produce compounds which are later washed away, leaving portions of the negative transparent.

To make a photograph, the negative is laid on a sheet of paper sensitized with a silver bromide suspension. When light is flashed on the negative, the paper beneath the transparent parts is illuminated, and that beneath the dark parts is shaded. In the developer, the silver bromine that was struck by light is reduced to metallic silver, creating the dark areas of the finished photograph. Thus, the photograph is a negative of the negative, or a *positive*. The dark areas of the original scene are reproduced as tones of black, and the light areas look white because the paper shows through its gelatin coating. After development, the positive is fixed, washed, and dried.

Photo: courtesy Eastman Kodak

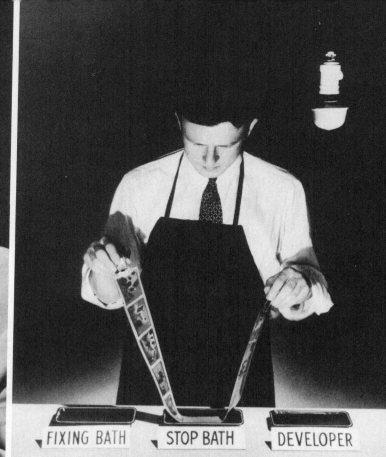

FIXING BATH   STOP BATH   DEVELOPER

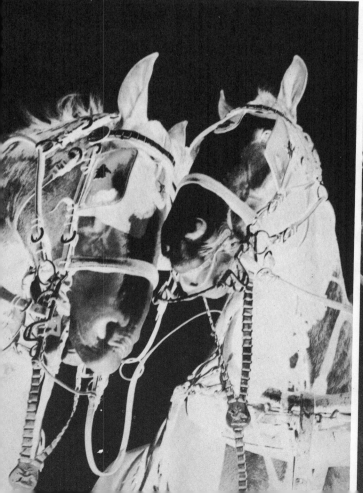

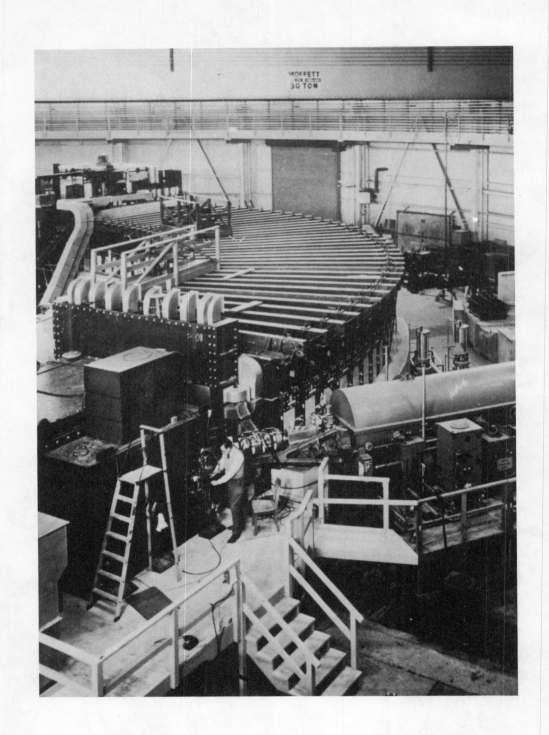

CHAPTER VIII

TOMORROW'S WORLD: THE POWER OF THE ATOM

THE BROAD FRONTIERS of science are a challenge to the keen and far-sighted men and women of this and future generations. In spite of the great progress which science has already experienced, there is every indication that we are on the brink of the greatest breakthrough of all times.

Our buildings are heated by a chemical reaction known as oxidation. This kind of reaction also powers our automobiles, airplanes, trains, and many machines. This kind of reaction also drives giant generators which produce the electricity that powers still other machines, and lights our homes, streets, and factories. But, oxidation releases only a tiny fraction of the energy that matter possesses.

For years, physicists have been trying to utilize more of the potential energy of matter. Finally, they have learned that by splitting atoms or initiating *nuclear fission,* we can obtain as much as three billion times the amount of energy released by chemical reactions!

Here is an introduction to the field of nuclear energy. While the subject is very complex, it is based on a few, easily-grasped fundamentals. Many of the problems of nuclear physics are yet unanswered. The potential usefulness of nuclear power is unlimited. With the promise of utility to mankind also comes the threat of destruction.

Photo: courtesy University of Calilfornia

NUCLEAR FISSION

MOST OF THE HEAT ENERGY used to power our machines and warm our buildings is obtained by chemical action. Oxidation, such as the burning of coal or oil, releases only about one 3-billionth of the potential energy that lies dormant in every piece of matter. Oxidation is a chemical reaction and therefore involves only the outermost electrons of the atoms. When the nucleus of an atom splits into two nearly-equal parts (a process called *nuclear fission*), almost three million times as much energy is released. One pound of fissionable material can release as much energy as 1,500 tons of coal.

An isotope of uranium, U_{235} (see page 14), is the most commonly used nuclear fuel. Fission is started by bombarding the U_{235} with neutrons. When a neutron penetrates the nucleus of a uranium atom, its kinetic energy upsets the delicate balance between the nuclear particles and causes the nucleus to divide into two parts of roughly the same size. As the fragments fly apart, they collide with nearby atoms causing them to move more rapidly, producing heat.

In addition to the nuclear fragments, each fission produces, on the average, two to three high-velocity neutrons. These neutrons may escape from the reacting mass or they may penetrate other uranium nuclei, causing them to fission in turn. When enough material is present so that at least one neutron produced by a fission strikes another atom and initiates a new fission, the action becomes a self-perpetuating *chain reaction*. The amount of material necessary to maintain a chain reaction is known as the *critical mass*. For uranium, it amounts to a few pounds.

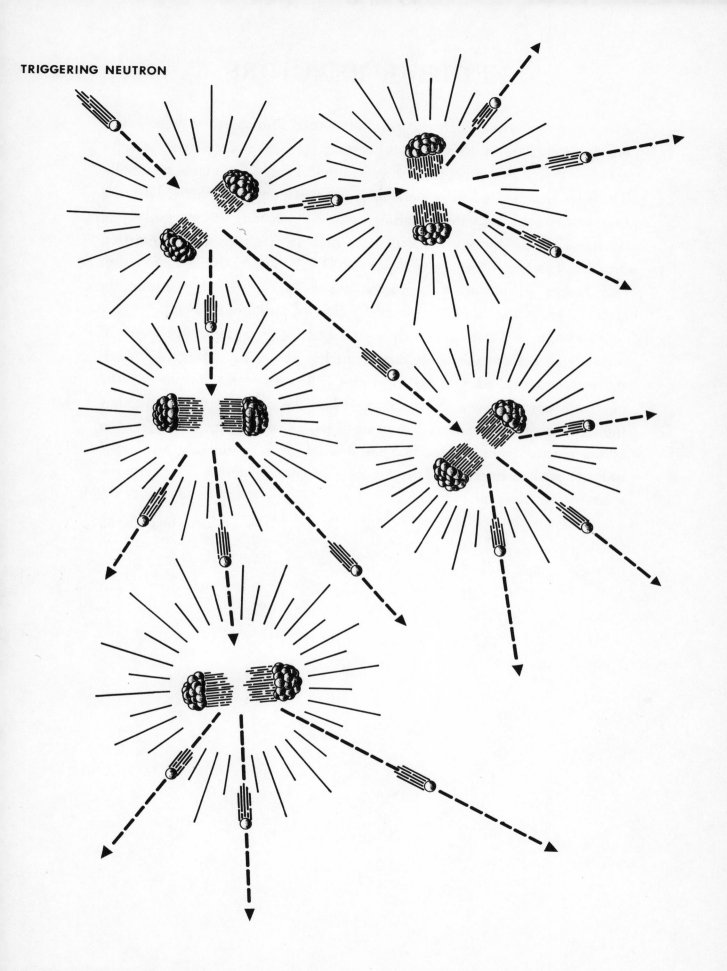

NUCLEAR REACTORS

Nuclear reactors or atomic piles are special "furnaces" in which heat energy is evolved by fission. The heart, or *core,* of a reactor consists of a number of hollow cylinders or slugs of nuclear fuel (fissionable material). The fuel is imbedded in a *moderator,* such as graphite, which slows the neutrons ejected from the fissioning atoms so that they are more likely to be taken up by another nucleus. The men in the picture are inserting uranium fuel slugs into a reactor at the Oak Ridge National Laboratory, Oak Ridge, Tennessee. This reactor, which has operated continuously since 1943, is the nation's principal source of radioisotopes.

The chain reaction in a reactor is regulated by means of a series of *control rods* composed of cadmium, a nuclear-absorbing substance. When the rods are pushed into the operating pile, they absorb some of the neutrons, slowing down the reaction. When the rods are pulled out, they intercept fewer neutrons and the rate of fission steadily increases. As soon as the reaction rate has reached the desired level, a sufficient number of rods are pushed into the pile to absorb just enough neutrons to keep the reaction rate constant.

Photo: courtesy Union Carbide

INDUSTRY AND THE ATOM

SEVERAL DESIGNS for nuclear-powered electric generating plants have been proposed. One of these designs is illustrated by this model and diagram. The velocity of the fragments produced by fission in the reactor corresponds to a temperature of about 600 billion degrees centigrade (one trillion degrees Fahrenheit). No way has yet been found to utilize this tremendous heat energy directly. Instead, a *coolant,* such as liquid sodium or water, is circulated through the reactor to absorb part of this heat. The coolant is then piped under high pressure to an exchanger, where it passes through coils surrounded by water at a lower pressure. As this water becomes heated, it changes to steam which is then used to operate a turbine. The turbine, in turn, powers a generator which produces electricity. The spent steam is cooled to its liquid state in the condenser and pumped back to the heat exchanger.

When their enormous energy content is considered, nuclear fuels are a fraction of the bulk and weight of other fuels and are consequently much easier to transport. This is particularly appealing to designers of ships and planes. Atomic-powered submarines have already been built which are capable of sailing around the world without stopping to refuel.

New, fissionable materials are an important by-product of the reactor. Thorium and normal uranium (U_{238}) are not fissionable in their natural state. But, when they are irradiated with neutrons, they are changed into fissionable isotopes that can be used as nuclear fuel.

Isotopes of many other elements can be produced by irradiation in a reactor. These isotopes are used in a number of interesting industrial processes. But, more important, is their great value to plant science, animal biology, and medicine.

Photo: courtesy Westinghouse

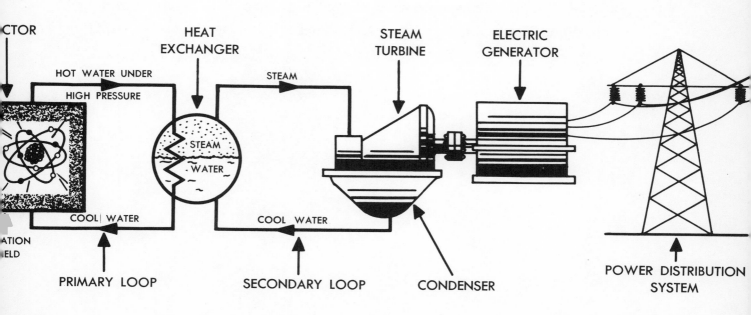

CTOR

ATION
ELD

HEAT
EXCHANGER

STEAM
TURBINE

ELECTRIC
GENERATOR

HOT WATER UNDER

HIGH PRESSURE

STEAM

STEAM

WATER

COOL WATER

COOL WATER

PRIMARY LOOP

SECONDARY LOOP

CONDENSER

POWER DISTRIBUTION
SYSTEM

PLANTS AND THE ATOM

SCIENTISTS are studying the effects of atomic radiation on plants in this experimental garden at the Brookhaven National Laboratory, New York. The source of radiation is a container of radioactive cobalt on the post in the center of the garden. Plants which are grown here are exposed to different radiation intensities, and for varying lengths of time. Exposure to atomic radiation has produced a number of interesting changes in the structure and functions of these plants and their offspring. The study of these changes led to a better understanding of the nature of plant life. Some of the discoveries may result in the development of better crop plants.

For many years, scientists have known which elements occur in plants and the proportion of plant tissue comprised by each. But they were not certain how the various elements entered the plant, nor did they understand the action of the elements within the plant.

Recently, however, plant scientists have learned to trace "tagged" atoms —radioactive isotopes which release small amounts of radiation—by the use of radiation-detecting devices, such as geiger counters. When a few tagged atoms are mixed with normal ones, the movement of an element can be followed from the soil, through the plant, until it is stored in tissue or discharged from the plant.

Atomic research has already led to many advances in our knowledge of plant life. These discoveries have been put to many practical uses, including the improvement of fertilizing techniques.

Photo: courtesy Brookhaven National Laboratory

ANIMALS AND THE ATOM

RADIOACTIVE ISOTOPES are revealing new facts about animals, too. For the first time, scientists can follow changes which occur in various chemicals from the instant they enter an animal's body until they leave it. The scientists in the picture are trying to determine how a cow manufactures milk. Radioactive isotopes have been added to the animal's food and injected into various parts of its body. Tracer elements are used by another group of scientists to study how hens make eggs. Scientists are also using tracers to follow the activities and bodily processes of mice, fish, flies, and other animals.

Tagged atoms are proving valuable in medicine. The discovery that iodine always collects in the thyroid gland led to the development of a new method of treating cancer of that organ. Radioactive iodine administered to a patient accumulates in the thyroid and its radiations kill the cancer cells. Scientists are now searching for chemicals that accumulate selectively in other organs of the body.

Research workers are also studying the harmful effect of radiation on the human body. Experiments which may cause malformations cannot be performed on humans. Therefore, scientists must study people who were irradiated during atomic blasts in World War II, or during accidental exposures since then. Much data valuable to medicine is also obtained by studying the effect of radiation upon other kinds of animals.

Photo: courtesy Union Carbide

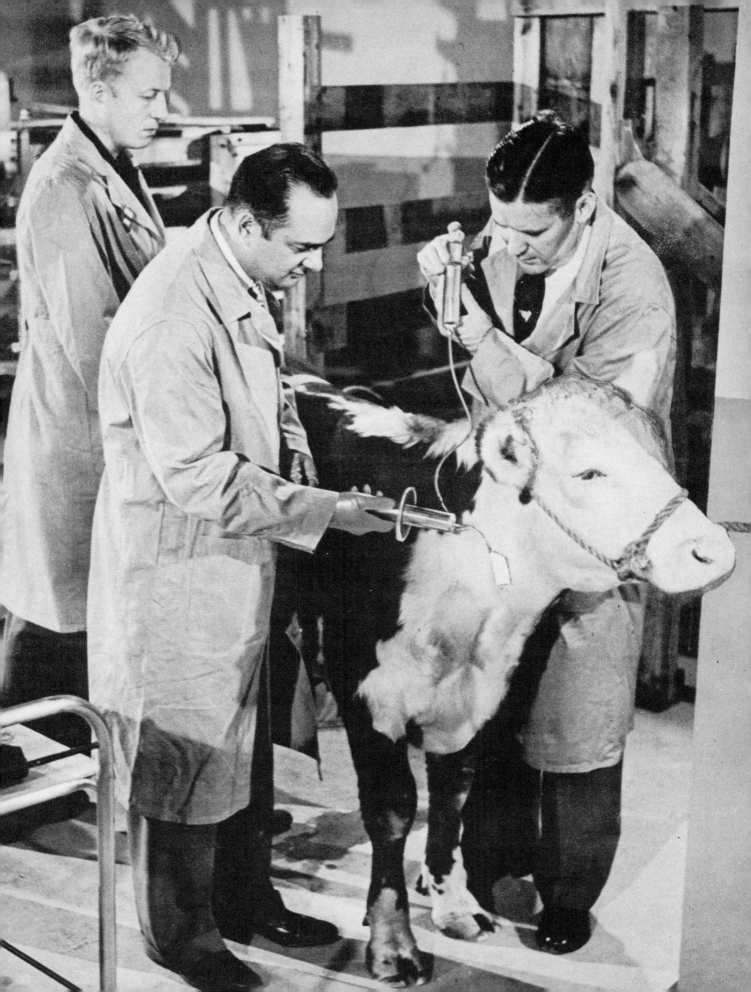

Index